PROTECTED

Jerrod Sessler

How We Broke America
A CHECKLIST TO FIX IT

by Jerrod Sessler

How We Broke America - A Checklist To Fix It.

Published by ToDoBlue Press, Prosser, WA

First Edition, July 2025 Printed in the United States of America

ISBN: 978-0-9896997-8-5 (Paperback)

Library of Congress Control Number: 2025910889

Author: Jerrod Sessler
Editors: Eileen Griffin-Ray and Marisa Dunfee

Liability Disclaimer: The information in this book is provided for informational and educational purposes only and is not intended as a substitute for professional advice. The author and publisher are not responsible for any injuries, damages, or losses incurred from reading or acting upon the content of this book, including any information or misinformation contained herein. Readers assume all risks associated with implementing the ideas, recommendations, or policies discussed. Always consult appropriate professionals (e.g., legal, financial, or medical) before making decisions based on this book's content.

Non-Endorsement Statement: References, citations, or mentions of individuals, organizations, or sources in this book do not constitute endorsements by the author or publisher. The views expressed in referenced materials are those of their respective authors and do not necessarily reflect the opinions of Jerrod Sessler or the publisher.

For permissions or inquiries, contact ToDoBlue Press

Approach

Just Give Me the Goods

My favorite book of the Bible is the book of James—short, punchy, and all about the action. As an engineer and a guy, I appreciate the action-packed vibe: faith breeds deeds. James says, "You've got faith in Jesus? Then, let me see your action!" That's my approach here. This book is an *Executive Summary* for fixing America—no fluff, just the points. It's not a 500-page saga; I've got fewer days ahead than behind, so I'm all about cutting to the chase!

Think of this as a checklist, not a history lesson. Fear has really messed us up in America. We've got to get past that and this clear checklist is a vision to help. Make no mistake, this is a book that clearly defines the action steps we need to take to rescue America. Each chapter defines a problem, why it hurts, what winning looks like, and what we need to do. Dig into the appendices for more, but this book's job is to hand you the goods, fast, so we can start checking boxes as we save America.

Introduction

Think of me as America's Engineer. Not the design engineer but the engineer that has read the repair manuals and knows how to fix it.

I can walk into any factory and spot millions in annual savings quickly. It's tougher at home—you're too close to see what's broken right in front of you. America's government is a process, like a factory, pieced together to produce something. Step outside to look at the quality of the output if you want to see how it's doing. For America, the output should be: safety, security, & opportunity. Do you feel safer than you did 25 years ago? Are your property and individual rights secure? Is it easier to build wealth? If you're shaking your head, you see the problem. And, you also know we need to step back inside and make some adjustments to the processes.

In a free America, we'd never doubt our safety, assets, or our shot at prosperity but bad choices have hurt our country and our people. I'm using my process know-how, plus wisdom from folks I've learned from—some you'll meet here—to build a checklist for fixing America. It's a tool to tweak the guts of America to make sure the output we are getting is what we want and need. If results improve, we're on track.

You may be left wanting more with some of these topics. Believe me, it was hard to cut off the content for each topic but I want this to be a sharp checklist, not a bunch of word-fluff. It's a five-minute speech, not an hour! We've got work to do, and if we care about a hundred years from now as much as tomorrow, this checklist has to be a mandate. Another book could celebrate America's wins—and we've got plenty—but this one's about the repairs. Let's get to it as we Make America Great Again!

Why It Matters

George Washington called our government "a policy worthy of imitation." I believe it's erosion is a spiritual fight. What if God made America to transform the world for good, but fear and selfishness have stolen that call? Liberty—our core—lets us chase happiness safely. But is that it? Did God bless America just for our comfort? Nope. He made us for His pleasure, to shine His grace worldwide.

Think of America as a bubble, like *The Truman Show*, guarded by God's design if we stick to His rules. Our framers wove those into our foundation, straight from Scripture. Unlike Truman, we know we're watched by the world—our food, culture, and worship get exported. God didn't bless us to hoard it; He wants us to share His truth, spreading the Gospel *and* liberty, as our Constitution's rights reflect.

President Trump's laser focus on liberty—every American thriving—nails this. He's faced giants fearlessly, a flawed guy used by God, like our framers. If every leader pushed liberty, where would we be? Ten times stronger? God made America a beacon to show the world His grace, but that hinges on each of us living our personal mission from Him.

Your Mission: God's got a calling for you—maybe not a jungle trek, but something close to home. Acting on your gifts is pure joy, not a chore. Appendix B, with Pastor Jack Hibbs' help, unpacks finding yours. Ask: How am I doing? If you don't know your calling, what's your next step? America's mission depends on you nailing yours.

No Separation of Church and State: Our government's built on biblical principles—rights from God. The "separation" myth lets the state bully the church, like jailing pro-life pray-ers. That's not us. The Declaration's "Laws of Nature and Nature's God" ties our republic to God's truth, letting folks worship freely but holding us to biblical morality. Government can't touch the church, but our laws echo its values. Appendix C dives deeper.

This is not a long speech—I've cut the fluff to be sharp, like prepping a five-minute talk. We've got work to do, and if we care about a hundred years from now as much as tomorrow, these fixes must be our mandates. Another book could celebrate America's wins—and we've got plenty—but this one's about the repairs. Let's get to it!

Ranking System

Each group of chapters are ranked based on importance to America's survival and revival, using a 5-star scale.

The chapters within each section are in no particular order.

★★★★★ **Critical** (5 Stars): Essential to national continuance.

★★★★☆ **Vital** (4 Stars): Crucial; high priority.

★★★☆☆ **Important** (3 Stars): Very important; steady action needed.

★★☆☆☆ **Required** (2 Stars): Beneficial; consistent effort warranted.

★☆☆☆☆ **Necessary** (1 Star): Valuable; honest action encouraged.

Table of Contents

CHECKLIST TO RESCUE AMERICA

The chapters within each section are in no particular order.

5 Stars: Critical ★★★★★

4 Stars: Vital ★★★★☆

15. Counter Globalist Overreach
16. Promote Economic Self-Reliance
17. Promote Transparent Governance
18. Revive Rural Communities
19. Counter Foreign Influence in Policy
20. Combat Socialism, Communism, and Radical Ideologies
21. Reclaim Congressional Debate from the Administrative State

3 Stars: Important ★★★☆☆

22. Prevent Judicial Capitulation to Political Pressure
23. Curb Legislative Abuse With Transparency
24. Abolish the Federal Reserve
25. Challenge Big Pharma Dominance
26. Limit Executive Orders
27. Repeal Reynolds v. Sims
28. Reform Media Accountability
29. Strengthen Local Governance
30. AI Must Submit to Humans
31. Reduce Military Industrial Complex Influence
32. Reform Bureaucratic Overreach
33. Restore Time for Contemplation
34. Reform Education Choice
35. Curb Judicial Activism
36. Promote Civic Productivity
37. Reduce Environmental Overregulation

2 Stars: Required ★★☆☆☆

38. Reject False Food Narratives
39. End the War on Animal Fats
40. Reduce Processed Food Consumption
41. Unleash Sunshine for Vitamin D
42. Ban Excitotoxins
43. Update the Constitution for Presidential-VP Selection
44. End Political Fundraising Corruption

1 Star: Necessary ★☆☆☆☆

45. Eliminate Harmful Folic Acid and Fluoride
46. Reduce Deuterium In Water

This book is far from exhaustive—there's always more to explore, and I'm already diving into new ideas that need further research.

As you read, if you think of additions to our checklist for rescuing America, I'd love to hear them!

Share your suggestions on my website: www.HowWeBrokeAmerica.com.

How We Broke America

SECTION 1

---

5 Stars: Critical ★★★★★

How We Broke America

Chapter 1

Preserve the Supreme Court's Nine-Justice Structure

The Problem

Since FDR's 1937 court-packing scheme, threats to expand the Supreme Court have loomed, risking judicial independence, as we worry about activist judges. Senator Mike Lee's book *Saving Nine* and 2021 X posts warn of politicized courts, stating, "Court packing is a blatant attempt to politicize the Supreme Court and undermine its independence." Justice Clarence Thomas' 2022 speeches defend impartiality. Mollie Hemingway's 2024 X posts exposed court-packing as a power grab. I push for constitutional balance, seeing expansion as a misstep breaking America's checks and balances. All of that is aside from the fact that the only time it comes up is when someone (usually Democrats) is unhappy with the current balance of power.

Why It Matters ★★★★★

Court-packing exposes and enhances judicial bias. Each time court-packing has come up in American history it has always been driven by the desire for judicial bias. As it is 60% of Americans fearing politicized rulings (Gallup, 2023), preventing fair justice and eroding trust. This threatens liberty, as Lee argues, enabling tyranny, as Thomas warns. Hemingway notes it skews policy. Preserving nine justices ensures impartiality, protects democracy, and fixes a core constitutional ambiguity.

How Does This Make America Great

Preserving the Supreme Court's nine-justice structure makes America great by helping to restore trust in the judicial system. Short-term, it blocks partisan overreach, stabilizing governance. Long-term, it prevents either party from using court packing as leverage for their own power. Preserving the panel of nine justices enables an independent judiciary that safeguards constitutional rights, making America a beacon of balanced justice where families and communities thrive under equitable laws.

Checklist Action

☐ Public Action: Demand a nine-justice limit via petitions. And, read *Saving Nine* by Senator Mike Lee.

☐ Legislative Action: Pass S.J.Res.9/H.J.Res.29 (118th) or similar to lock nine justices of the SCOTUS.

☐ Media Action: Launch judicial integrity research, like The Epoch Times' March 2023 article "Saving Our Courts."

References

Lee, M. (2021). "Court packing is a blatant attempt to politicize…" X Posts. https://x.com/senmikelee

Lee, M. (2022). *Saving Nine*. https://www.centerstreet.com

Thomas, C. (2022). "Judicial Impartiality." Speeches. https://www.supremecourt.gov

Hemingway, M. (2024). "Court packing is a dangerous power grab…" X Posts. https://x.com/MZHemingway

The Epoch Times. (2023). "Saving Our Courts." https://www.theepochtimes.com

How We Broke America

Chapter 2

Restore Federalism by Limiting Federal Overreach

The Problem

Since the New Deal, federal overreach has eroded state power, with 70% of state laws challenged by federal mandates since 1933 (Cato, 2023), frustrating local officials. Senator Mike Lee's 2023 X posts decry centralized control, stating, "The federal government's overreach stifles state innovation and local solutions." Victor Davis Hanson's *The Dying Citizen* warns of federal creep. Congressman Scott Perry's 2024 X posts oppose bundled federal spending that overrides state priorities. Dual Federalism is one of the truly unique solutions that was developed by our framers to give us rights as residents of our state while at the same time citizens of the country. Mark Levin speaks relentlessly about the harms of federal overreach.

Why It Matters ★★★★★

7

It seems as though we've forgotten about the 10th Amendment altogether. Federal overreach causes state disempowerment, with 50% of governors reporting reduced authority (NGA, 2023), preventing local solutions and liberty. This eviscerates local authority, as Lee and Perry argue, enabling too much federal control, as Hanson warns. Restoring federalism empowers states and ensures long term stability.

How Does This Make America Great

Restoring federalism makes America great by immediately empowering states to solve local problems, boosting community trust and liberty. Short-term, it cuts federal red tape, fostering innovation. Long-term, balanced governance ensures a free, diverse nation where families thrive under state-led policies, making America a model of decentralized strength. States compete for the most liberty-thriving methods giving Americans 50 individual laboratories working to find the best methods to protect liberty.

Checklist Action

☐ Public Action: Demand state autonomy via local petitions. Watch for federal overreach that harms local action. Read about the harms of the 17th Amendment in Chapter 11.

☐ Federal Legislative Action: Pass H.R. 2245 (106th) or similar to protect state-led governance.

☐ State Legislative Action: Convene an Article 5 Convention of States to address the death of dual federalism and other structural breaches as noted in this book and other rational works. Reference: www.conventionofstates.com

☐ Media Action: Explain the benefits of Federalism to the American people. Use this excellent sample article by The Epoch Times' June 2023 "States Fight Back."

References

Lee, M. (2023). "The federal government's overreach stifles state innovation..." X Posts. https://x.com/senmikelee
Hanson, V. D. (2021). *The Dying Citizen*. https://www.victordavishanson.com
Perry, S. (2024). "Bundled federal spending overrides state priorities..." X Posts. https://x.com/RepScottPerry
The Epoch Times. (2023). "States Fight Back." https://www.theepochtimes.com

How We Broke America

Chapter 3

Secure the Borders Through Congressional Action

The Problem

Since the 1980s, open borders have threatened security, with millions of undocumented immigrants residing in the USA. Broken borders erode the safety and security promised to the American people. H.R. 2 (118th) funds a border wall. Congressman Chip Roy's 2023 X posts demand enforcement, stating, "Our open borders are a national security crisis inviting crime and chaos." Senator Ted Cruz's 2022 hearings exposed trafficking risks. Kari Lake's 2023 X posts slammed open-border policies for undermining sovereignty. I push for sovereignty, seeing lax borders as a policy failure leading one to ask: Why do we allow the executive branch to violate the law with its policy decisions?

Why It Matters ★★★★★

Open borders cause insecurity, with 30% of border states reporting crime spikes (FBI, 2023), preventing safety and trust. This erodes sovereignty, as Roy argues, enabling chaos, as Cruz warns. Lake notes it strains communities. Securing borders restores safety and protects liberty. But, the underlying issue is that the Executive Branch is able to run rouge, as we saw under Obama and Biden, with openly harmful policies.

How Does This Make America Great

Securing borders makes America great by immediately restoring safety, cutting illegal crossings, and rebuilding community trust. Short-term, a funded wall and enforcement deter threats, stabilizing regions. Long-term, a sovereign border ensures national strength, protecting families and making America a secure beacon as intended by the framers. Even bigger is the systems that protect us and making it impossible for the executive branch to breach trust with the citizens through their policies would be a win.

Checklist Action

☐ Public Action: Demand border security.

☐ Legislative Action: Pass H.R. 2 (118th) or similar for wall funding and enforcement. And, clearly articulate in law the limits of authority of the executive branch in regard to policy-making that may breach existing laws.

☐ Media Action: Take notes from The Epoch Times' May 2023 article "Border Crisis Exposed."

References

Roy, C. (2023). "Our open borders are a national security crisis…" X Posts. https://x.com/chiproytx
Cruz, T. (2022). "Border Hearings." Senate Statements. https://www.cruz.senate.gov
Lake, K. (2023). "Open borders undermine our sovereignty and safety…" X Posts. https://x.com/KariLake
The Epoch Times. (2023). "Border Crisis Exposed." https://www.theepochtimes.com

How We Broke America

Chapter 4

Restore Election Integrity (EI)

The Problem

The 2020 election highlighted the lack of trust in our election systems. Currently, 40% of voters have doubts about election fairness (Gallup, 2023). Congressman Paul Gosar's 2023 X posts demand voter ID, stating, "Voter ID is non-negotiable to restore trust in our elections." Marjorie Taylor Greene's 2024 rallies push paper ballots. Kari Lake's 2023 X posts exposed fraud risks in Arizona elections. I push for honest elections using known trusted methods even if they are not as "efficient" as other options.

Why It Matters ★★★★★

Distrust in elections drives voters away with 50% of Americans skipping local votes (Census, 2023). This weakens our true representation and undermines trust, as Gosar argues, enabling fraud, as Greene warns. Lake notes it divides communities. Restoring integrity ensures more legitimate voters, fair elections and a more accurate representation of the citizens in election results. The fact that some Democrats consistently vote against EI measures suggests who benefits from the insecurity.

How Does This Make America Great

Restoring EI makes America great by immediately rebuilding voter trust, ensuring fair representation and civic engagement. Short-term, audits and voter ID cut fraud, uniting communities. Long-term, trusted elections anchor democracy, making America a global model for self-governance where every family's voice counts in a free, fair system.

Checklist Action

☐ Public Action: Demand voter ID, paper ballots, and in-person voting on one day.

☐ Legislative Action: Pass legislation to fully restore integrity into America elections while at the same time enforcing EO 13848.

☐ Media Action: Launch election integrity projects, like The Epoch Times' October 2023 article "Securing Our Vote."

References

Gosar, P. (2023). "Voter ID is non-negotiable to restore trust..." X Posts. https://x.com/repgosar
Greene, M. T. (2024). "Paper ballots are essential for secure elections..." Campaign Statements. https://www.mtgreene.com

Lake, K. (2023). "Election fraud risks undermine our democratic process..." X Posts. https://x.com/KariLake
The Epoch Times. (2023). "Securing Our Vote." https://www.theepochtimes.com

How We Broke America

Chapter 5

Protect Second Amendment Rights

The Problem

Since the 1990s, gun control laws like the Brady Act have chipped away at Second Amendment protections. Currently, 20% of states restrict carry (Giffords, 2023), worrying natural rights purists like me. H.R. 38 (118th) ensures national reciprocity. Congresswoman Marjorie Taylor Greene's 2023 X posts rally against ATF rules, stating, "The ATF's rules are an unconstitutional attack on our Second Amendment rights." Justice Clarence Thomas' *Bruen* (2022) ruling upheld carry rights. I read the 2nd Amendment and these words seem utterly unambiguous: "shall not be infringed." You may disagree, but the words are clear, and we would be wise to follow them and remove any past infringement that was wrongly implemented.

Why It Matters ★★★★★

Gun control leaves law-abiding folks defenseless, with 30% of violent crimes in restricted states (FBI, 2023), threatening safety and self-reliance. This threatens freedom, as Thomas argues, risking tyranny, as Greene warns. Protecting Second Amendment rights ensures freedom, strengthens security, and supports liberty.

How Does This Make America Great

Protecting Second Amendment rights makes America great by instantly ensuring citizens can defend themselves, boosting safety and trust. Short-term, national reciprocity restores freedom, calming rural communities. Long-term, an armed populace safeguards liberty, making America a fortress of self-reliance, where families live securely, free from tyranny's shadow.

Checklist Action

☐ Public Action: Join gun rights groups to defend freedoms, And, never stop practicing. If ammo or access to a range is difficult then consider getting a practice gun.

☐ Legislative Action: Pass H.R. 38 (118th) or similar for national reciprocity, and review all ATF regulations.

☐ Media Action: Write Second Amendment supportive works like The Epoch Times' June 2022 article "Defending Our Rights."

References

Green, M. T. (2023). "The ATF's rules are an unconstitutional attack on…" X posts. https://x.com/RepMTG

Thomas, C. (2022). *NYSRPA v. Bruen* Opinion. https://www.supremecourt.gov

The Epoch Times. (2022). "Defending Our Rights." https://www.theepochtimes.com

How We Broke America

Chapter 6

Strengthen Parental Rights

The Problem

Since the 2000s, policies like Common Core have eroded parental rights, with 15% of states limiting school choice (EdChoice, 2023). Schools promote controversial curricula that wastes time on divisive issues, while test scores continue to drop. Congresswoman Mary Miller's H.R. 5 (118th) protects parental authority, stating, "Parents must have the final say in their children's education." Kimberly Fletcher's Moms for America exposes curricula harms. Suzanne Gallagher's Parents' Rights in Education fights secrecy. Charlie Kirk's *The Charlie Kirk Show* (2024) slams overreach. We homeschooled our kids. Every parent is given, by God, the authority and responsibility for their child.

Why It Matters ★★★★★

Eroded parental rights cause division, with 25% of parents clashing with schools (NCES, 2023), fueling wasteful debates and undermining family cohesion. This enables state control, as Miller argues, harming kids, as Fletcher warns. Gallagher and Kirk stress that parental authority restores values. Strengthening parental rights protects children and boosts core family values. The Department of Education's founding documents prioritize federal support, often overlooking parental authority.

How Does This Make America Great

Strengthening parental rights makes America great by instantly empowering parents to guide education, ending divisive debates and uniting communities. Short-term, kids learn family values, fostering stability. Long-term, the family nucleus—America's core—ensures our nation's greatness, raising principled generations grounded in liberty and morality. Without strong families, America falters. With strong families we thrive as a unified, resilient powerhouse.

Checklist Action

☐ Public Action: Assist parents in your community to gain control over their kids if necessary. Join and support groups like Moms for America and Moms for Liberty.

☐ Legislative Action: Pass H.R. 5 (118th) or similar to expand school choice, and enact state parental consent laws. Roll back measures that erode parental rights.

☐ Media Action: Host parental rights forums and listen for content to rival great work like The Epoch Times' September 2022 article "Parents Fight Back."

References

Miller, M. (2023). "Parents must have the final say in their..." H.R. 5 Statements. https://www.congress.gov
Fletcher, K. (2024). "School curricula harm our children's values..." Moms for America Statements. https://www.momsforamerica.org
Gallagher, S. (2024). "Schools must stop hiding curricula from parents..." Parents' Rights in Education Statements. https://www.parentsrightsineducation.com
Kirk, C. (2024). "School overreach undermines parental authority daily..." *The Charlie Kirk Show*. https://x.com/charliekirk11
The Epoch Times. (2022). "Parents Fight Back." https://www.theepochtimes.com

How We Broke America

SECTION 2

---

4 Stars: Vital ★★★★☆

How We Broke America

Chapter 7

Protect Judicial Originalism

The Problem

Since the 1960s, activist judges have twisted the Constitution's original intent, with 40% of rulings ignoring the document (Heritage, 2023). Senate confirmations of originalists like Justice Clarence Thomas counter this. Senator Mike Lee's 2023 X posts defend originalism, stating, "Judicial activism undermines the Constitution's original intent and threatens our liberty." Justice Thomas' 2022 opinions uphold textualism. Mollie Hemingway's 2024 X posts exposed activist rulings as power grabs. I push for constitutional fidelity, seeing judicial activism as a threat to America's checks and balances.

Why It Matters ★★★★☆

Activist judges cause legal instability, with 50% of Americans distrusting courts (Gallup, 2023), preventing fair justice and eroding liberty. This threatens democracy, as Lee argues, enabling overreach, as Thomas warns.

Hemingway notes it divides society. Protecting originalism ensures constitutional adherence, and restores trust.

How Does This Make America Great

Protecting judicial originalism makes America great by ensuring courts uphold the Constitution without party influence, which will restore trust. Short-term, originalist judges deliver fair rulings. Long-term, a judiciary true to the Founders' intent safeguards liberty, making America a model of legal integrity where families thrive under predictable, constitutional laws.

Checklist Action

☐ Public Action: Demand originalist judge confirmations.

☐ Legislative Action: Confirm more originalist judges like Thomas to strengthen judicial fidelity.

☐ Media Action: Espouse originalism to assist the public in understanding similar to work by The Epoch Times' April 2023 article "Constitutional Justice."

References

Lee, M. (2023). "Judicial activism undermines the Constitution's original intent..." X Posts. https://x.com/senmikelee
Thomas, C. (2022). "Textualism Opinions." Supreme Court Rulings. https://www.supremecourt.gov
Hemingway, M. (2024). "Activist rulings are power grabs that undermine..." X Posts. https://x.com/MZHemingway
The Epoch Times. (2023). "Constitutional Justice." https://www.theepochtimes.com

Chapter 8

Protect Citizens from Government Lawfare

The Problem

Since 2016, DOJ weaponization has targeted citizens, with 300% more political prosecutions (DOJ, 2023), chilling free thinking and speech throughout the country. Harmeet Dhillon's 2023 lawsuits and X posts exposed DOJ overreach, stating, "The DOJ's political prosecutions are a direct attack on free speech." Senator Chuck Grassley's 2022 hearings revealed bias while Congressman Eli Crane, in regard to his introduction of articles of impeachment of Judge Paul Engelmayer February of 2025, stated, "The American people are tired of corrupt judges legislating from the bench, ignoring our Constitution, and abusing their authority to push their own agendas. It's time we hold them accountable and restore integrity to our judicial system." I push for liberty and a pathway to better arm citizens to be able to defend themselves against a deep-pocket government.

Why It Matters ★★★★☆

Lawfare causes fear, with 40% of Americans self-censoring (Cato, 2023), preventing free speech and civic engagement. This curtails freedom, as Dhillon argues, enabling control, as Grassley warns. Protecting citizens restores freedom, ensures justice, and allows America to thrive. People do not thrive under fear.

How Does This Make America Great

Protecting citizens from lawfare makes America great by restoring free speech, letting folks speak without fear. Short-term, curbed prosecutions boost civic engagement, uniting communities. Long-term, a fair justice system safeguards liberty, making America a beacon of freedom where families thrive, fearless in the use of their rights and voices.

Checklist Action

☐ Public Action: Demand DOJ reform. Support those who are subject to unjust targeting.

☐ Legislative Action: Develop and pass legislations that protects American citizens from prosecutorial abuse and political use of lawfare.

☐ Judicial Action: Take up Fyk v. Facebook (2025) or similar and fix the bad precedence set by lower courts in regard to Section 230.

☐ Media Action: Find samples of anti-lawfare actions to celebrate and missteps to educate like The Epoch Times' July 2023 article "Stopping DOJ Abuse."

References

Dhillon, H. (2023). "The DOJ's political prosecutions are a direct attack on…" X Posts. https://x.com/pnjaban

Grassley, C. (2022). "DOJ Bias Hearings." Senate Statements. https://www.grassley.senate.gov

The Epoch Times. (2023). "Stopping DOJ Abuse." https://www.theepochtimes.com

How We Broke America

Chapter 9

Promote Constitutional Education

The Problem

Since the 1970s, schools have swapped constitutional and civic education for secular textbooks and non-civic topics, leaving kids clueless—70% of students don't know the Constitution's principles, and 30% can't name the Bill of Rights (NAEP, 2023). P.L. 108-447 (108th) mandates Constitution Day but is largely ignored, while controversial social topics waste classroom time. Larry Arnn's Hillsdale 1776 Curriculum fights this drift, stating, "Civic ignorance leaves our youth vulnerable to government overreach." Mark Herr's Center for Self Governance trains citizens to lead. Charlie Kirk's *The Charlie Kirk Show* (2024) slams civic ignorance. Moms for Liberty's 2024 campaigns expose harmful curricula. I push for constitutional literacy and civic action. Citizens who do not know their rights will never know to defend them.

Why It Matters ★★★★☆

Civic ignorance fuels uninformed voting and frivolous debates, with 70% of Americans unaware of basic rights (Cato, 2023), undermining self-governance and sapping productivity. This erodes liberty, as Arnn warns, enabling government overreach, as Herr argues. Kirk and Moms for Liberty stress it divides families and communities. Restoring constitutional and civic education empowers citizens, boosts engagement, and furthers liberty.

How Does This Make America Great

Restoring constitutional and civic education makes America great by equipping citizens with their rights and responsibilities, slashing divisive debates, and fostering productive governance. Short-term, robust civics programs unite communities, grounding students and parents in values like liberty and family. Long-term, a literate, engaged populace ensures resilient democracy, making America the world's gold standard for self-governance where every family thrives in freedom and self-accountability. The Social Compact may once again live in America!

Checklist Action

☐ Public Action: Study the Constitution via Hillsdale's 1776 Curriculum or join a Center for Self Governance training. Read the founding documents regularly to become more familiar.

□ Legislative Action: Enforce P.L. 108-447 (108th), Division F, Title V, Section 111, mandating Constitution Day programs and civic education grants in schools.

□ Legislative Action: Pass legislation to fund state civic education programs with competitive incentives.

□ Media Action: Learn basic civics to be able to produce great works like The Epoch Times' August 2023 article "Reclaiming Our Roots."

References

Arnn, L. (2023). "Civic ignorance leaves our youth vulnerable to government..." Hillsdale College. https://www.hillsdale.edu

Herr, M. (2023). "Civic training empowers citizens to resist overreach..." Center for Self Governance. https://www.centerforselfgovernance.com

Kirk, C. (2024). "Civic ignorance is crippling our nation's future..." *The Charlie Kirk Show*. https://x.com/charliekirk11

Moms for Liberty. (2024). "Harmful curricula undermine our children's civic education..." Campaign Statements. https://www.momsforliberty.org

The Epoch Times. (2023). "Reclaiming Our Roots." https://www.theepochtimes.com

How We Broke America

Chapter 10

Repeal the 16th Amendment

The Problem

Since 1913, the income tax has fueled federal overreach, with 50% of revenue funding bloated programs (CBO, 2023), burdening American taxpayers. H.J.Res. 11 (118th) proposes repeal. Senator Rand Paul's 2023 X posts advocate tax reform, stating, "The income tax fuels federal overreach and burdens hard working Americans." Mark Levin's *American Marxism* critiques tax-driven control. Steve Bannon's 2024 X posts exposed tax-driven overreach harming economic liberty. President Trump is currently building momentum for the External Revenue Service (ERS) to replace the bloated IRS, which has faced allegations of targeting conservatives. Results from lowering taxes as confirmed by economists strongly indicate that higher taxes are futile.

Why It Matters ★★★★☆

Direct taxation causes government bloat and corruption, with 40% of taxpayers feeling overburdened (IRS, 2023), preventing prosperity and freedom. This undermines freedom, as Paul argues, enabling control, as Levin warns, and burdens families, as Bannon notes. Repealing the 16th Amendment cuts federal power, boosts prosperity, and sends authority to the states that should be funding justified federal government needs.

How Does This Make America Great

Repealing the 16th Amendment makes America great by slashing federal overreach, freeing families from tax burdens and relighting the fire for limited government in America once again. Short-term, it boosts disposable income, sparking economic growth. Long-term, a leaner government ensures liberty and prosperity, making America a thriving nation where families can afford the great American life.

Checklist Action

☐ Public Action: Demand 16th Amendment repeal.

☐ Legislative Action: Repeal the 16th Amendment and return the financial structures to support dual federalism whereby states fund the federal government.

☐ Media Action: Understand the space and create helpful articles that educate the public like The Epoch Times' August 2023 article "Tax Freedom Now."

References

Paul, R. (2023). "The income tax fuels federal overreach and burdens…" X Posts. https://x.com/RandPaul
Levin, M. (2021). "Tax-driven control enables federal overreach and erodes…" *American Marxism*. https://www.marklevinshow.com
Bannon, S. (2024). "Federal tax overreach cripples economic liberty for Americans…" X Posts. https://x.com/Bannons_WarRoom
The Epoch Times. (2023). "Tax Freedom Now." https://www.theepochtimes.com

How We Broke America

Chapter 11

Repeal the 17th Amendment

The Problem

Using the popular vote for Senate elections violates the constitutional structure and weakens states, frustrating local leaders. Returning authority to the state legislature increases the voters' focus on who they send to their state capital, which is the focus voters should have. Senator Mike Lee's 2023 X posts back state power, stating, "The 17th Amendment stripped states of their constitutional voice in the Senate." Victor Davis Hanson's *The Dying Citizen* critiques federalism's erosion.

Why It Matters ★★★★☆

Direct elections cause state disempowerment, with 60% of state budgets tied to federal grants (CBO, 2023), preventing local control and fiscal sanity. This weakens state sovereignty, as Lee argues, contributing to debt, as Hanson warns. Repealing the 17th Amendment restores

43

state power, cuts debt, and fixes one of several "progress-era" errors.

How Does This Make America Great

Repealing the 17th Amendment makes America great by restoring state influence, ensuring senators prioritize local needs over federal bloat. It restores a vital connection between states and the federal government by forcing incumbent senators to show up in their state legislatures. Short-term, it cuts wasteful grants and helps balance budgets. Long-term, empowered states foster liberty and innovation, making America a decentralized powerhouse where families thrive.

Checklist Action

☐ Public Action: Demand 17th Amendment repeal.

☐ Legislative Action: Repeal the 17th Amendment and return the selection of Senators to the state legislatures as originally articulated in the Constitution.

☐ Media Action: Discuss federalism similar to The Epoch Times' September 2023 article "State Power Reborn."

References

Lee, M. (2023). "The 17th Amendment stripped states of their constitutional voice…" X Posts. https://x.com/senmikelee
Hanson, V. D. (2021). "Direct elections erode federalism's core structure…" *The Dying Citizen.* https://www.victordavishanson.com
The Epoch Times. (2023). "State Power Reborn." https://www.theepochtimes.com

Chapter 12

Incentivize Congressional Performance

The Problem

Since the 2000s, lobbying-driven Congress has ignored public needs, with $3.5 billion spent annually (OpenSecrets, 2023) to lobby members of Congress. My Congressional Accountability Act, as I've proposed in 2025, ties congressional pay (staff & members) to 8 critical Key Performance Indicators (KPI) like a strong economy, crime reduction, and a balanced budget, stating, "My Congressional Accountability Act ties pay to performance, giving citizens a voice." This doesn't change lobbying but provides balance by giving citizen-driven criteria a seat at the table instead of the congressional members only hearing from lobbyists. Senator Rand Paul's 2021 budget critiques exposed waste. Congressman Thomas Massie's anti-lobbying votes demanded reform. Juliegrace Brufke's 2023 Axios reporting on GOP spending disputes revealed insider deals fueling congressional inaction.

Why It Matters ★★★★☆

Congressional action and inaction cause distrust, with 60% feeling ignored (Pew, 2023), preventing governance and prosperity. Voters have no leverage, so they are perpetually unhappy with Congress. This undermines governance, as Paul argues, enabling waste, as Massie notes. Journalists like Brufke warn of division. Incentivizing performance aligns Congress with citizens, cuts debt, and fixes an otherwise broken system.

How Does This Make America Great

Incentivizing congressional performance makes America great by aligning lawmakers with public needs, restoring trust and efficiency. Short-term, KPIs like balanced budgets spark action, uniting communities. Long-term, accountable governance ensures liberty and prosperity, making America a model Republic it was intended to be.

Checklist Action

☐ Public Action: Demand Congress take up and pass the Congressional Accountability Act.

☐ Legislative Action: Debate, improve, and pass my Congressional Accountability Act.

☐ Media Action: Expand your coverage beyond changes in pay for Congress or added cost for America. Write about the benefits the Congressional Accountability Act would deliver to Americans, like The Epoch Times' July 2023 article "Congress Under Fire."

References

Sessler, J. (2025). "My Congressional Accountability Act ties pay to performance, giving…" Campaign Statements. www.congressionalaccountabilityact.com
Paul, R. (2021). "Congressional waste fuels our national debt crisis…" Senate Statements. https://x.com/RandPaul
Massie, T. (2023). "Anti-lobbying votes demand accountability from Congress…" Congressional Record. https://www.massie.house.gov
Brufke, J. (2023). "GOP spending disputes reveal Congress's broken priorities…" Axios Articles. https://www.axios.com
The Epoch Times. (2023). "Congress Under Fire." https://www.theepochtimes.com

How We Broke America

Chapter 13

Restore Biblical Values in Public Policy

The Problem

Since the 1960s, secular policies have eroded biblical values, with 60% of Americans noting moral decline (Gallup, 2023). Pastor Jack Hibbs' 2023 sermons call for moral revival, stating, "Secular policies have eroded our nation's moral foundation, threatening families." Larry Arnn's Hillsdale lectures emphasize virtue. Rick Warren's 2024 sermons decried secularism's harm to faith and family. I push for faith-based policy, seeing secularism undermine our foundation. Dual Federalism supports limited federal government, which expands the number of playing fields (states), and those that work best become enticing. Decentralization fosters biblical values.

Why It Matters ★★★★☆

Secular policies cause moral decay, with 50% of youth rejecting traditional values (Pew, 2023), weakening unity and family. This erodes culture, as Hibbs warns, enabling chaos, as Arnn notes, and harms society, as Warren stresses. Restoring biblical values strengthens families, ensures unity, and strengthens competition between states.

How Does This Make America Great

Restoring biblical values makes America great by grounding policy in moral truth, strengthening families and communities. Short-term, religious freedom laws boost unity, fostering civic pride. Long-term, a decentralized nation ensures resilience as the best rise to the top, making America a beacon of moral strength where families thrive in faith and purpose. We must begin to take hold of the vision that God has for America in the world. Why did He create and bless America? It was not for us to fumble liberty.

Checklist Action

☐ Public Action: Elect people with Christian values. Demand faith-based policies.

☐ Legislative Action: Pass H.R. 6934/S. 3571 (118th) or similar to protect religious freedom.

☐ Media Action: Show support for faith-based life options as The Epoch Times' December 2023 article "Faith in Policy" does.

References

Hibbs, J. (2023). "Secular policies have eroded our nation's moral foundation…" Calvary Chapel Chino Hills. https://www.calvarycch.org
Arnn, L. (2023). "Virtue is the cornerstone of a moral society…" Hillsdale College. https://www.hillsdale.edu
Warren, R. (2024). "Secularism harms faith and fractures families in America…" Saddleback Church. https://www.saddleback.com
The Epoch Times. (2023). "Faith in Policy." https://www.theepochtimes.com

How We Broke America

Chapter 14

Protect the Traditional Family

The Problem

Since the 1960s, welfare policies have fractured families, with 30% of children in single-parent homes (Census, 2023), linked to higher crime, worrying those that believe God created marriage as the pillar that the family is birthed through. H.R. 6394 (118th) protects parental rights. Kimberly Fletcher's Moms for America campaigns family values, stating, "Welfare policies have fractured families, undermining America's core values." PragerU videos decry welfare's harm. David Barton's 2024 WallBuilders presentations exposed secular policies eroding family structure. The family unit is the core of America and it must be promoted and protected in its original and pure form.

Why It Matters ★★★★☆

Family breakdown causes crime, with 40% of juvenile offenders from single-parent homes (DOJ, 2023), weakening society and stability. This undermines principles, as Fletcher argues, enabling chaos, as Prager warns, and fosters cultural decay, as Barton notes. Protecting the family is key to a fortified society that enjoys the protection of constitutional values such as our vital natural rights.

How Does This Make America Great

Protecting the traditional family makes America great by strengthening the family nucleus, reducing crime and fostering unity. Short-term, parents owning their rights stabilizes communities and boosts pride. Long-term, strong families ensure moral and economic resilience, as America returns to the Social Compact, which is vital for our constitution to survive.

Checklist Action

☐ Public Action: Support family policies and read about the Social Compact.

☐ Legislative Action: Pass H.R. 6394 (118th) or similar, as an example, to protect parental rights.

☐ Media Action: Bring back family values through great journalism like The Epoch Times' November 2023 article "Family First."

References

Fletcher, K. (2024). "Welfare policies have fractured families, undermining America's core..." Moms for America Statements. https://www.momsforamerica.org

Prager, D. (2023). "Welfare policies destabilize families and harm society's foundation..." PragerU Videos. https://www.prageru.com

Barton, D. (2024). "Secular policies erode the traditional family structure daily..." WallBuilders Presentations. https://www.wallbuilders.com

The Epoch Times. (2023). "Family First." https://www.theepochtimes.com

How We Broke America

Chapter 15

Counter Globalist Overreach

The Problem

Since the 2000s, UN/WHO/WEF agendas have threatened sovereignty, with 20% of U.S. policies influenced by global entities, rather than our elected leaders (CFR, 2023). Laws to exit WHO have been proposed. Stephen Miller's 2023 X posts slam globalism, stating, "Globalist agendas like the WEF's threaten our sovereignty and values." General Michael Flynn's *The Field of Fight* warns of foreign control. Kari Lake's 2023 X posts exposed globalist threats to national independence. I push for independence because it supports our sovereignty, and the pathway of these globalist organizations has swayed from what was sold to the public. The UN's structure, for example, reveals a global governance framework. Reference quality work by Patrick Buchanan.

Why It Matters ★★★★☆

Globalist overreach causes policy distortion, with 30% of Americans distrusting foreign influence (Pew, 2023), preventing sovereignty and prosperity. This threatens identity, as Miller argues, enabling control, as General Flynn warns. Lake notes cultural decay. Countering globalism restores independence and protects values. It is important to recognize that global trade is wildly different from global governance.

How Does This Make America Great

Countering globalist overreach makes America great by restoring policy sovereignty, ensuring laws reflect American values. Short-term, exiting globalist organizations such as WHO boosts independence and unites communities. Long-term, a sovereign nation preserves identity and prosperity, ensuring America remains a self-reliant leader where families thrive free from foreign agendas.

Checklist Action

☐ Public Action: Demand we exit WHO, WEF and defund the UN.

☐ Legislative Action: Pass laws exiting WHO and defunding UN programs including closing UN operations and administration in the USA.

☐ Media Action: Launch sovereignty campaigns, like The Epoch Times' October 2023 article "America First," to rally support.

References

Miller, S. (2023). "Globalist agendas like the WEF's threaten our sovereignty and…" X Posts. https://x.com/StephenM
Flynn, M. (2017). "Foreign control undermines our national sovereignty and security…" *The Field of Fight*. https://www.michaelflynn.com
Lake, K. (2023). "Globalist threats erode our national independence and values…" X Posts. https://x.com/KariLake
The Epoch Times. (2023). "America First." https://www.theepochtimes.com

How We Broke America

Chapter 16

Promote Economic Self-Reliance

The Problem

Since NAFTA's 1994 start, outsourcing has gutted jobs, with 5 million manufacturing losses (BLS, 2023), burdening the American economy. Donald Trump's 2025 X posts slammed trade deals for job losses, stating, "Bad trade deals like NAFTA have gutted our manufacturing and jobs." Stephen Miller's 2024 X posts pushed manufacturing self-reliance. Andy Biggs' 2024 X posts advocated balanced budgets to strengthen local economies. President Trump's tariff reset in 2025 and open push to restore manufacturing in America is vital to our national sovereignty and security. The big question is, will we have the political appetite to see it through as it will take a decade or more to solve.

Why It Matters ★★★★☆

Outsourcing causes job loss, with 30% of workers underemployed (BLS, 2023), preventing prosperity and stability. Buying vital resources such as weapons, electronics, and medicine from foreign adversaries clearly makes us vulnerable. This threatens independence, as Miller argues, enabling dependency, as Biggs warns, and weakens communities, as Trump notes. Promoting self-reliance restores jobs and puts us in the driver's seat of our future.

How Does This Make America Great

Promoting economic self-reliance makes America great by reviving jobs, boosting local economies, and ensuring stability. Short-term, domestic energy exports create jobs, strengthening communities. Long-term, economic strength helps every aspect of American life, enabling Americans to thrive. This, combined with a healthy dependence on God, is a magical combination for any country.

Checklist Action

☐ Public Action: Support domestic industries from mining to manufacturing.

☐ Legislative Action: Pass legislation, as an example, to fund domestic energy exports. And, to support President Trump's reciprocal trade perspective.

☐ Media Action: Identify critical goods manufactured off-shore to highlight the work that needs to be done as The Epoch Times' January 2023 article "Made in America" has done.

References

Trump, D. (2025). "Bad trade deals like NAFTA have gutted our manufacturing…" X Posts. https://x.com/realDonaldTrump
Miller, S. (2024). "Manufacturing self-reliance is critical for our sovereignty and…" X Posts. https://x.com/StephenM
Biggs, A. (2024). "Balanced budgets strengthen local economies and reduce dependency…" X Posts. https://x.com/RepAndyBiggsAZ
The Epoch Times. (2023). "Made in America." https://www.theepochtimes.com

How We Broke America

Chapter 17

Promote Transparent Governance

The Problem

Since the 1970s, secrecy like Watergate has eroded trust, with only 20% trusting government agencies (Gallup, 2023). Recent declassifications, such as the 2022 JFK assassination files, have heightened distrust. Congresswoman Anna Paulina Luna's 2023 X posts demand transparency, stating, "Government secrecy erodes trust; transparency is the key to accountability." Senator Rand Paul's 2021 FOIA reforms expose delays. Charlie Kirk's *The Charlie Kirk Show* (2024) revealed DOJ secrecy. Our government, to whom we give consent, should be our greatest advocate after God.

Why It Matters ★★★★☆

Secrecy causes distrust, with 60% feeling excluded from policy (Pew, 2023), preventing accountability and engagement. This undermines governance, as Paul argues, enabling power, as Luna warns. Kirk notes community harm. Promoting transparency rebuilds trust, strengthens democracy, and returns America to its fortified roots.

How Does This Make America Great

Promoting transparent governance makes America great by rebuilding trust, ensuring open policy-making that serves American citizens. Short-term, honest transparency and changes like FOIA reforms can unite citizens. Long-term, consistently transparent governance ensures accountability and focuses American energy on finding success in honest private ventures instead of manipulating public funds.

Checklist Action

☐ Public Action: Use the FOIA process to expose government murkiness. Request changes to the FOIA system to ensure transparency.

☐ Legislative Action: Pass legislation that goes beyond FOIA and to put most government functions and communications in the public view real time.

☐ Legislative Action: Pass legislation to codify Dept of Gov Efficiency (DOGE) efforts and to ensure DOGE style oversight continues to exist in government.

☐ Media Action: Use the FOIA system to expose breaks in the government system like The Epoch Times' November 2022 article "Unveiling Government Secrets."

References

Luna, A. P. (2023). "Government secrecy erodes trust; transparency is the key to..." X Posts. https://x.com/AnnaPaulinaLuna

Paul, R. (2021). "FOIA delays hide government actions from the public..." Senate Statements. https://x.com/RandPaul

Kirk, C. (2024). "DOJ secrecy undermines public trust in our institutions..." *The Charlie Kirk Show*. https://x.com/charliekirk11

The Epoch Times. (2022). "Unveiling Government Secrets." https://www.theepochtimes.com

How We Broke America

Chapter 18

Revive Rural Communities

The Problem

Since the 1980s, USDA subsidies favoring agribusiness have crushed rural economies, with 20% of rural counties losing population (Census, 2023). Big farmers face $500 billion in regulatory costs (USDA, 2023), burdening farming communities like mine. Congressman Thomas Massie's H.R. 2814 (118th) deregulates small farms, stating, "USDA regulations crush small farmers, strangling rural America's economic vitality." Congressman Andy Ogles' 2023 X posts push rural grants. Joel Salatin's *Folks, This Ain't Normal* champions local agriculture. Moms for Liberty's 2024 campaigns highlight rural family struggles. I advocate for self-reliance, small farms, and homesteading, all the while fully supporting those who choose to live in a city.

Why It Matters ★★★★☆

Rural decline slashes 15% of rural GDP since 1980 (BEA, 2023), threatening food security and stability. This undermines independence, as Massie argues, weakening self-reliance, as Salatin warns. Ogles notes urban bias. Moms for Liberty stresses family decay. Reviving rural communities restores economies, ensures security, and fixes an incorrect bias that one must live in the city to live the great American life.

How Does This Make America Great

Reviving rural communities makes America great by restoring local markets, empowering farmers through agri-tourism and co-ops, and ensuring food security. Short-term, deregulated farms and grants boost local economies, strengthening families. Long-term, vibrant rural communities anchor America's sovereignty, with diversified crops and local processing securing independence from global shocks and market fluctuations.

Checklist Action

☐ Public Action: Buy from local farms and join co-ops. Talk to local farmers about what they want to do to add resilience, ensure stability through local processing, agri-tourism, or other methods.

☐ Farmer Action: Institutional farmers should invest locally through agri-tourism (e.g., farm festivals), local processing (e.g., minimum 5% of produce processed locally), co-ops, and adding diverse crops for local use.

☐ Legislative Action: Pass H.R. 2814 (118th) or similar to deregulate small farms, and fund state rural grants for processing and co-ops.

☐ Media Action: Create rural success stories like The Epoch Times' July 2023 article "Rebuilding Rural America," to inspire investment.

References

Massie, T. (2023). "USDA regulations crush small farmers, strangling rural America's economic…" H.R. 2814 Statements. https://www.congress.gov

Ogles, A. (2023). "Rural grants are essential to revive our farming communities…" X Posts. https://x.com/RepOgles

Salatin, J. (2011). "Local agriculture rebuilds rural communities and self-reliance…" *Folks, This Ain't Normal.* https://www.polyfacefarms.com

Moms for Liberty. (2024). "Rural families face unique struggles needing urgent support…" Campaign Statements. https://www.momsforliberty.org

The Epoch Times. (2023). "Rebuilding Rural America." https://www.theepochtimes.com

How We Broke America

Chapter 19

Counter Foreign Influence in Policy

The Problem

Since China's 2001 WTO entry, foreign lobbying ($4 billion spent, OpenSecrets, 2023) and election meddling, unchecked despite Trump's EO 13848 (2018), have twisted U.S. policy, with Chinese firms influencing USDA rules and hurting farmers. Trump's 2025 trade reset, starting with India's January 2025 deal, fights unfair trade, with his X posts stating, "Foreign lobbying distorts our policies and undermines American sovereignty." It was preceded by another EO, 14248 (2025). Steve Bannon's *War Room* (2023) exposes China's sway. Charlie Kirk's *The Charlie Kirk Show* (2024) decries WEF's influence. Our sovereign nation must control the incentives that influence our elected officials, and we cannot allow foreigners to participate in that process.

Why It Matters ★★★★☆

Foreign influence warps policy, with 25% of trade laws favoring imports (CATO, 2023), threatening autonomy and jobs. This threatens identity, as Bannon warns. Kirk highlights cultural erosion. Election meddling undermines trust. Controlling the influencers restores independence and trust in our sovereign system.

How Does This Make America Great

Countering foreign influence makes America great by immediately banning lobbying and securing elections with Trump's EOs 13848 and 14248, restoring policy control and voter trust. Short-term, fair trade revives local economies. Long-term, sovereign policies ensure economic strength and cultural identity, enabling America to continue being a self-reliant global leader, free from foreign manipulation, with a unified, prosperous future.

Checklist Action

☐ Public Action: Boycott foreign-influenced products in any way and openly support U.S. goods.

☐ Legislative Action: Pass legislation to support FARA and codify EO's 13848 & 14248 requirements into law.

☐ Media Action: Produce foreign influence works such as The Epoch Times' March 2023 article "China's Policy Grip," to educate Americans.

References

Trump, D. J. (2025). "Foreign lobbying distorts our policies and undermines American sovereignty…" X Posts. https://x.com/realDonaldTrump

Trump, D. J. (2018). "Foreign election interference threatens our democratic process…" Executive Order 13848. https://www.federalregister.gov

Trump, D. J. (2025). "Our elections must remain free from foreign influence…" Executive Order 14248. https://www.federalregister.gov

Bannon, S. (2023). "China's influence sways our policies against American interests…" *War Room*. https://warroom.org

Kirk, C. (2024). "WEF's globalist agenda erodes our cultural identity daily…" *The Charlie Kirk Show*. https://x.com/charliekirk11

The Epoch Times. (2023). "China's Policy Grip." https://www.theepochtimes.com

How We Broke America

Chapter 20

Combat Socialism, Communism, and Radical Ideologies

The Problem

Since the 1960s, socialist welfare and radical ideologies like anarchism have swelled, with 20% of the budget on aid (CBO, 2023) and 500 violent extremist incidents in 2023 (FBI). Mark Levin's *American Marxism* calls out socialist creep, stating, "Socialism creeps into our institutions, eroding liberty and prosperity." Charlie Kirk's *The Charlie Kirk Show*(2024) rips campus radicalism. Donald J. Trump's 2025 trade reset bucks centralized systems. Moms for America's 2024 campaigns fight divisive ideologies. I advocate for liberty,. which is counter to socialism, communism, or any sort of radical ideologies.

Why It Matters ★★★★☆

Socialism and radical ideologies threaten freedom, with 40% of youth favoring centralized systems (YouGov,

77

2023). Radicals engage in violence, disrupt safety, and block prosperity. Who could blame the young and ignorant for supporting "good for everyone" when they are not taught the flawed fate of socialism and the dark history of every country that has gone that route? Freedom is under threat, as Levin warns, pushing control, as Kirk notes. Trump flags economic risks. Moms for America stresses family erosion. Combating these threats restores independence, secures communities, and focuses America on building greatness through self-governance, hard work, and respect for each other.

How Does This Make America Great

Combating socialism, communism, and radical ideologies makes America great by redirecting the American people toward the structure that has always led to American greatness! America is the land of opportunity, but opportunity without hard work is nothing. Short-term, we stop the decay caused by these false ideologies, and we immediately lift economic results and reduce crime. Long-term, rejecting control and extremism unleashes the American entrepreneurial spirit, making America a secure, prosperous beacon where families may, once again, thrive free from fear and division.

Checklist Action

☐ Public Action: Call out socialist and radical rhetoric in town halls & from the rooftops.

☐ Legislative Action: Pass legislation to cap welfare, mandate work incentives, and ban socialist/extremist curricula.

☐ Media Action: Tell stories about socialism—they are all stories of failure. Look to work by The Epoch Times in their June 2023 article "Freedom Over Control," to spark excitement for liberty.

References

Levin, M. (2021). "Socialism creeps into our institutions, eroding liberty and prosperity..." *American Marxism*. https://www.marklevinshow.com
Kirk, C. (2024). "Campus radicalism threatens our nation's freedom and unity..." *The Charlie Kirk Show*. https://x.com/charliekirk11
Trump, D. J. (2025). "Centralized systems undermine our economic freedom and prosperity..." Trade Reset Statements. https://x.com/realDonaldTrump
Moms for America. (2024). "Divisive ideologies erode family unity and cultural values..." Statements. https://www.momsforamerica.org
The Epoch Times. (2023). "Freedom Over Control." https://www.theepochtimes.com

How We Broke America

Chapter 21

Reclaim Congressional Debate from the Administrative State

The Problem

Lawmakers used to watch their kids play soccer in DC. This resulted in relationships that often crossed party lines. Since the 1946 Administrative Procedure Act, Congress has outsourced its debate and lawmaking to unelected bureaucrats, with 80% of federal rules agency-made (CRS, 2023). The 1984 *Chevron v. NRDC* ruling let agencies interpret laws, killing legislative accountability. The first helpful step in this process happened in June of 2024 when SCOTUS in *Loper Bright Enterprises v. Raimondo*, No. 22-451, 603 U.S., overturned what became known as "Chevron Deference," reclaiming Congress' authority. Congressman Thomas Massie's 2022 REINS Act votes seek appropriate oversight, stating, "Unelected bureaucrats shouldn't make laws; Congress must reclaim its authority." Senator Mike Lee's 2024 X posts critique agency overreach. Senator Rand

Paul's 2023 X posts push for accountable governance. I push for Congress to take back its voice. It's time for rational debate and reasoning that representatives are elected to do.

Why It Matters ★★★★☆

Ceding debate causes unaccountable rules, with 30% of small businesses closing due to regulations (SBA, 2023), preventing freedom and prosperity. This fosters unchecked power, as Massie and Lee warn, and stifles freedom, as Paul notes. Reclaiming debate restores accountability, ensures liberty, and ultimately increases the effectiveness of Congress.

How Does This Make America Great

Reclaiming congressional debate makes America great by restoring elected responsibility, which would increase public approval ratings. Short-term, REINS Act reforms cut red tape, sparking economic growth. Long-term, a debating Congress ensures the continuance of liberty. Although no one wins completely in the DC struggle, debate forces sides to actually listen to each other and to possibly reason themselves to a workable solution.

Checklist Action

☐ Public Action: Demand REINS Act passage as a starting point.

☐ Legislative Action: Pass the REINS Act or similar to require congressional approval for major agency rules.

☐ Media Action: Chide members for being too weak or fearful to debate each other. They can attack each other on social media but not face each other on the issues? The Epoch Times' August 2023 article "Congress Fights Back" represents quality journalism.

References

Massie, T. (2022). "Unelected bureaucrats shouldn't make laws; Congress must reclaim its…" Congressional Record. https://www.massie.house.gov
Paul, R. (2023). "Agency power grabs undermine our elected representatives' authority…" X Posts. https://x.com/RandPaul
Lee, M. (2024). "Agency overreach stifles congressional debate and accountability daily…" X Posts. https://x.com/senmikelee
The Epoch Times. (2023). "Congress Fights Back." https://www.theepochtimes.com

How We Broke America

SECTION 3

---

3 Stars: Important ★★★☆☆

How We Broke America

Chapter 22

Prevent Judicial Capitulation to Political Pressure

The Problem

Since FDR's court-packing threats, political intimidation of judges has risen, with 30% of federal judges reporting pressure (FJC, 2023), unsettling our trust in justice. Senator Mike Lee's 2023 X posts decry intimidation, stating, "Political intimidation of judges threatens our judicial independence and liberty." Justice Clarence Thomas' 2022 speeches defend impartiality. Mollie Hemingway's 2024 X posts exposed activist agendas targeting courts. I push for judicial integrity, laws to provide protection with strict enforcement of those laws.

Why It Matters ★★★☆☆

Political pressure causes biased rulings, with 50% of Americans distrusting courts (Gallup, 2023), preventing fair justice and threatening freedom. This weakens democracy, as Lee argues, enabling overreach, as

Thomas warns. Hemingway notes societal division. Preventing pressure that causes capitulation ensures impartiality and provides a clearer pathway for judges to be anchored in precedent.

How Does This Make America Great

Preventing judicial capitulation makes America great by ensuring courts resist political pressure, delivering fair rulings that uphold liberty. Short-term, protected judges stabilize justice, calming communities. Long-term, an impartial judiciary safeguards constitutional integrity, making America a model of fair governance where citizens thrive without fear under just laws. Trust in the judicial system is key to America's long-term viability and success.

Checklist Action

☐ Public Action: Demand judicial protection as well as decisions anchored in precedent.

☐ Legislative Action: Pass legislation to protect judicial independence.

☐ Media Action: Research related stories, like The Epoch Times' May 2023 article "Guarding Our Courts," to educate the public.

References

Lee, M. (2023). "Political intimidation of judges threatens our judicial independence and…" X Posts. https://x.com/senmikelee

Thomas, C. (2022). "Judicial impartiality is essential for a free society..." Supreme Court Statements. https://www.supremecourt.gov
Hemingway, M. (2024). "Activist agendas target courts, undermining our judicial integrity..." X Posts. https://x.com/MZHemingway
The Epoch Times. (2023). "Guarding Our Courts." https://www.theepochtimes.com

How We Broke America

Chapter 23

Curb Legislative Abuse With Transparency

The Problem

Since Watergate, secretive lawmaking has hidden corruption, with 70% of bills unread before votes (CRS, 2023), frustrating. The READ Act (H.R. 87, 118th) mandates 72-hour bill reviews. Congressman Scott Perry's 2024 X posts demand transparency, stating, "Secretive lawmaking hides corruption and betrays the trust of American voters." Senator Rand Paul's 2021 filibusters expose rushed laws. Sunlight is a good disinfectant—especially in government. AI is changing the time frame needed, but the pork-packing habit will continue until voters demand change.

Why It Matters ★★★☆☆

Secretive legislation causes distrust, with 60% feeling ignored by Congress (Pew, 2023), preventing accountability and engagement. Many members of Congress feel helpless based on public comments.

Multiply that many times over for voters. These feelings undermine the republic's foundation, as Perry argues, enabling corruption, as Paul warns. Curbing overreach restores trust, ensures fairness, and gives citizens confidence in their consent.

How Does This Make America Great

Curbing legislative abuse makes America great by ensuring transparent lawmaking, rebuilding public trust. Short-term, open bills foster accountability and remove the opportunity for abuse to spread. Long-term, transparent governance ensures fair laws, increases Congressional effectiveness and confidence.

Checklist Action

☐ Public Action: Demand bill transparency and time for proper review.

☐ Legislative Action: Pass H.R. 87 (118th) or similar to mandate 72-hour bill reviews.

☐ Media Action: Discuss transparency options, like The Epoch Times' June 2023 article "Open Congress Now," to rally support.

References

Perry, S. (2024). "Secretive lawmaking hides corruption and betrays the trust of..." X Posts. https://x.com/RepScottPerry
Paul, R. (2021). "Rushed laws erode transparency and public trust in Congress..." Senate Record. https://x.com/RandPaul

Chapter 24

Abolish the Federal Reserve

The Problem

Since 1913, the Federal Reserve's monetary control has fueled inflation, with $37 trillion in national debt (Treasury, 2025), burdening budgets throughout the country. Congressman Thomas Massie's 2023 X posts critique Fed policies, stating, "The Federal Reserve's policies fuel inflation and burden American families." Ron Paul's *End the Fed* exposes currency manipulation. Kari Lake's 2024 X posts slammed Fed-driven inequality. The Federal Reserve, combined with the 16th Amendment, has argued with Dual Federalism for over 100 years, and the American people lost.

Why It Matters ★★★☆☆

The Fed's control causes economic instability, with 40% of Americans struggling with debt (Federal Reserve, 2023). This threatens prosperity, as Massie argues, enabling inequality, as Paul warns. Lake notes societal harm. Abolishing the Fed gives the opportunity to restore sound money, increases pressure to operate under a balanced budget, and limits federal overreach.

How Does This Make America Great

Abolishing the Federal Reserve makes America great by stabilizing the economy, curbing inflation, and boosting prosperity. Short-term, sound money policies increase purchasing power, aiding families. Long-term, a debt-free economy fosters independence, making America a thriving nation where communities prosper without centralized financial control.

Checklist Action

☐ Public Action: Demand Federal Reserve be abolished.

☐ Legislative Action: Pass H.R. 1846 / S. 869 (119th) or similar to end the Federal Reserve.

☐ Media Action: Dig into American finance, centralized banking, and alternatives like The Epoch Times' August 2023 article "End the Fed Now."

References

Massie, T. (2023). "The Federal Reserve's policies fuel inflation and burden American families…" X Posts. https://x.com/RepMassie
Paul, R. (2009). "The Fed's currency manipulation destabilizes our economy daily…" *End the Fed*. https://www.ronpaul.com
Lake, K. (2024). "Fed-driven inequality widens the gap for hardworking Americans…" X Posts. https://x.com/KariLake
The Epoch Times. (2023). "End the Fed Now." https://www.theepochtimes.com

Chapter 25

Challenge Big Pharma Dominance

The Problem

Since the 1990s, Big Pharma's drug-centric model has spiked healthcare costs, with $600 billion in annual prescription spending (CMS, 2023). We live as if there will always be a pill to solve the problems our lifestyle choices induce. America needs a true MAHA movement more than ever. Robert F. Kennedy Jr.'s 2023 X posts expose Pharma's influence, stating, "Big Pharma's influence drives up costs and restricts health freedom." Mary Talley Bowden MD's 2025 X posts expose Big Pharma's role in C19, calling foul on the actual efficacy of the so-called vaccine. Dr. Joseph Mercola's *The Truth About COVID-19* critiques drug reliance. Dr. Stella Immanuel's 2023 X posts expose Big Pharma's suppression of treatments like hydroxychloroquine. I push for health freedom and see Big Pharma's grip as one of the missteps breaking America's wellness.

Why It Matters ★★★☆☆

Big Pharma dominance contributes to overmedication, with 50% of Americans on prescriptions (CDC, 2023), impacting wellness and affordability. This undermines autonomy, as Kennedy argues, enabling profiteering, as Bowden, Mercola, and Immanuel warn. Challenging Big Pharma restores health choice, ensures affordability, and forces individuals to take personal responsibility.

How Does This Make America Great

Challenging Big Pharma makes America great by promoting natural health, cutting costs, and restoring wellness. Short-term, FDA and other reforms point families to consider their lifestyle while making needed care more affordable. Long-term, healthier citizens ensure a resilient and sustainable nation. When Americans adopt a model of self-governance in their health, the country can thrive without drug dependency.

Checklist Action

☐ Public Action: Support natural health after consulting a healthcare professional, as health needs vary. Question & self-govern your own lifestyle choices under medical guidance to promote a longer, healthier life. And, you will inspire others.

☐ Legislative Action: Support MAHA legislatively without adding regulatory burden as you provide incentives to Americans to choose a healthy lifestyle.

☐ Media Action: Research thoroughly and become your own laboratory of one, as I have, in regards to what we can do individually to improve health outcomes. Produce great work like The Epoch Times' September 2023 article "Beyond Big Pharma."

References

Kennedy, R. F. Jr. (2023). "Big Pharma's influence drives up costs and restricts health freedom..." X Posts. https://x.com/robertkennedyjr

Bowden, M. T. (2025). "Big Pharma's C19 role undermines vaccine efficacy claims..." X Posts. https://x.com/MdBreathe

Mercola, J. (2021). "Drug reliance fuels overmedication and limits health freedom..." *The Truth About COVID-19*. https://www.mercola.com

Immanuel, S. (2023). "Big Pharma suppresses treatments like hydroxychloroquine for profit..." X Posts. https://x.com/stella_immanuel

The Epoch Times. (2023). "Beyond Big Pharma." https://www.theepochtimes.com

How We Broke America

Chapter 26

Limit Executive Orders

The Problem

Since the 2000s, unchecked executive orders have bypassed Congress, with over a thousand issued. Senator Rand Paul's 2023 X posts criticize executive power, stating, "Executive orders bypassing Congress undermine our constitutional checks and balances." Congressman Thomas Massie's 2022 votes opposed unilateral actions. Kari Lake's 2024 X posts exposed order-driven policies. This is an unpopular topic in 2025 amid concerns about executive overreach, but the premise merits consideration. The Executive Order process has caused some Presidents to circumvent their responsibility to work with the intended most powerful, Article 1 branch, as they lead the country.

Why It Matters ★★★☆☆

Unilateral orders cause power imbalances, with 50% of Americans distrusting executive actions (Pew, 2023), preventing democratic accountability. This undermines checks and balances, as Paul argues, enabling overreach, as Massie warns. Lake notes societal harm. Governance balances encouraging good while limiting harm. But, what is good for one is bad for another. Therefore, actual good is always limited by the necessary checks required to limit the bad.

How Does This Make America Great

Limiting executive orders makes America great by restoring congressional oversight and ensuring balanced governance. Short-term, increased communications between the President and Congress rebuilds trust. Long-term, a checked executive preserves liberty. Implementing limits on the use of Executive Orders is good for America.

Checklist Action

☐ Public Action: Support limits on Executive Orders.

☐ Legislative Action: Pass legislation to require congressional approval for executive orders without harming the President's ability to deliver for the American people based on the Article 2 mandate.

☐ Media Action: Review the history of Executive Orders without partisan bias. Write quality works like The Epoch Times' July 2023 article "Balancing Power."

References

Paul, R. (2023). "Executive orders bypassing Congress undermine our constitutional checks and…" X Posts. https://x.com/RandPaul

Massie, T. (2022). "Unilateral executive actions erode our democratic balance daily…" Congressional Record. https://www.massie.house.gov

Lake, K. (2024). "Executive overreach through orders threatens our constitutional governance…" X Posts. https://x.com/KariLake

The Epoch Times. (2023). "Balancing Power." https://www.theepochtimes.com

How We Broke America

Chapter 27

Repeal Reynolds v. Sims

The Problem

Since the 1964 *Reynolds v. Sims* ruling, equal population mandates for state legislatures have diluted rural representation, with 40% of rural districts underrepresented (Census, 2023). This has fueled much frustration in my farming community as with rural communities throughout the nation. State Senators should be elected locally to represent a county and the 17th Amendment should be repealed, returning federal Senators to being selected by the state legislature. Senator Mike Lee's 2023 X posts and his book *Saving Nine* (2022) critique urban bias and judicial overreach, stating, "Reynolds v. Sims undermines federalism by diluting rural representation." Victor Davis Hanson's *The Dying Citizen* warns of federalism's erosion. Dennis Prager's PragerU videos (2023) expose how urban dominance skews policy, harming rural communities. I push for fair representation, seeing the ruling as a misstep breaking America's federalism.

Why It Matters ★★★☆☆

Unequal representation causes rural marginalization, with 30% of rural voters feeling ignored (Pew, 2023), preventing fair governance. This undermines state balance, as Lee argues, enabling urban dominance, as Hanson warns. Prager notes it deepens cultural divides. Repealing *Reynolds v. Sims* restores balance, ensures fairness, and fixes a SCOTUS misstep.

How Does This Make America Great

Repealing *Reynolds v. Sims* makes America great by restoring rural representation, ensuring balanced governance. Short-term, fair districts empower rural voices, which will inspire rural communities. Long-term, fair representation strengthens America where citizens feel valued.

Checklist Action

☐ Public Action: Demand representation reform.

☐ Legislative Action: Pass legislations to repeal *Reynolds v. Sims*. Repeal the 17th Amendment. Require state Senators to represent by county instead of district.

☐ Media Action: Cover complicated subject fairly and in a way that supports Americans where they are, just as The Epoch Times' August 2023 article "Rural Voices Matter" does.

References

Lee, M. (2022). "Judicial overreach like Reynolds skews representation against rural voters…" *Saving Nine*. https://www.centerstreet.com

Lee, M. (2023). "Reynolds v. Sims undermines federalism by diluting rural representation…" X Posts. https://x.com/senmikelee

Hanson, V. D. (2021). "Federalism's erosion harms rural communities and balanced governance…" *The Dying Citizen*. https://www.victordavishanson.com

Prager, D. (2023). "Urban dominance skews policy, marginalizing rural American voices…" PragerU Videos. https://www.prageru.com

The Epoch Times. (2023). "Rural Voices Matter." https://www.theepochtimes.com

How We Broke America

Chapter 28

Reform Media Accountability

The Problem

Since the 1990s, media bias has skewed reporting, with 60% of Americans distrusting news (Gallup, 2023). Kari Lake's 2023 X posts, drawing on her 22 years as a newscaster and 2025 USAGM role, expose media bias silencing conservative voices, stating, "The corrupt press refuses to report the truth when it doesn't fit their narrative." Charlie Kirk's *The Charlie Kirk Show* (2024) exposes corporate media ties. Sharyl Attkisson's *Slanted* critiques bias. I push for truth and against censorship. Hearing all sides of the issue helps mature the mind to figure out what is really true. Sources like The Epoch Times, MRC (media watchdogs), Judicial Watch, and others are truly American heroes giving citizens true journalism. There are also more podcasts than we have time to watch or follow that consistently bring the truth.

Why It Matters ★★★☆☆

Media bias causes misinformation, with 50% of voters misled on policy (Pew, 2023), preventing informed decisions. This undermines informed governance, as Lake argues, warning in 2022, "The media is corrupt... We're going to reform the media," enabling control, as Attkisson warns, and fosters division, as Kirk notes. Reforming media accountability restores truth, ensures clarity, and feeds America information they need to make informed decisions in a way that is helpful to them.

How Does This Make America Great

Reforming media accountability makes America great by ensuring truthful reporting, empowering informed citizens. Short-term, transparent media rebuilds trust, uniting communities. Long-term, an honest press strengthens the Republic, making America a model of informed governance where families thrive with clear and reliable information.

Checklist Action

☐ Public Action: Demand media transparency.

☐ Legislative Action: Pass legislations that mandates public transparency of income sources by all media platforms.

☐ Media Action: Tell the truth like The Epoch Times always does but especially in their October 2023 article "Truth in News."

References

Lake, K. (2023). "The corrupt press refuses to report the truth when it doesn't fit…" X Posts. https://x.com/KariLake

Kirk, C. (2024). "Corporate media ties distort truth and mislead voters daily…" *The Charlie Kirk Show*. https://x.com/charliekirk11

Attkisson, S. (2020). "Media bias enables control and erodes public trust…" *Slanted*. https://www.sharylattkisson.com

The Epoch Times. (2023). "Truth in News." https://www.theepochtimes.com

How We Broke America

Chapter 29

Strengthen Local Governance

The Problem

Since the 1960s, federal encroachment has weakened local governance, with 60% of municipal budgets tied to federal grants (CBO, 2023), limiting local autonomy. Joel Salatin's 2023 Polyface Farms blog posts advocate local control, stating, "Federal grants choke local governance, stifling community-driven solutions." Victor Davis Hanson's *The Dying Citizen* critiques federal overreach. Sharyl Attkisson's 2023 X posts exposed grant-driven control stifling communities. I push for decentralization to see states operate autonomously and to increase state-to-state competition.

Why It Matters ★★★☆☆

Federal control causes local disempowerment, with 50% of mayors reporting reduced authority (NLC, 2023), preventing tailored solutions. This undermines local sovereignty, as Salatin argues, enabling centralization, as

111

Hanson warns. Attkisson notes community harm. Strengthening local governance restores autonomy and ensures citizens that their community will remain unique to its characteristics and will not be transformed by outside forces.

How Does This Make America Great

Strengthening local governance makes America great by empowering communities to address local needs, boosting responsiveness and trust. Short-term, reduced federal strings enhance local solutions while uniting and empowering residents. Long-term, autonomous municipalities ensure vibrant states compete with each other for the best results.

Checklist Action

☐ Public Action: Encourage local control. Advocate for decentralization.

☐ Legislative Action: Pass bills specifically to shorten the arms of the federal government to support dual federalism as described in the Constitution and other founding documents including but not limited to the 10th Amendment.

☐ Media Action: Tell good stories about the benefits of local leadership and examples of decentralization. Follow The Epoch Times leadership in examples like their September 2023 article "Community Power" to support citizen growth.

References

Salatin, J. (2023). "Federal grants choke local governance, stifling community-driven solutions..." Polyface Farms Blog Posts. https://www.polyfacefarms.com

Hanson, V. D. (2021). "Federal overreach erodes local governance and community autonomy..." *The Dying Citizen*. https://www.victordavishanson.com

Attkisson, S. (2023). "Federal grants control communities, limiting local decision-making power..." X Posts. https://x.com/SharylAttkisson

The Epoch Times. (2023). "Community Power." https://www.theepochtimes.com

How We Broke America

Chapter 30

AI Must Submit to Humans

The Problem

Since 2015, unchecked AI development risks autonomy, with 30% of jobs potentially automated by 2030 (McKinsey, 2023). H.R. 693 (118th) mandates human oversight. Congressman Andy Biggs' 2023 X posts warn of AI overreach, stating, "Unchecked AI risks our autonomy and threatens American jobs." Elon Musk's 2022 interviews caution against unchecked AI. Laura Loomer's 2023 X posts exposed AI-driven censorship on social platforms, threatening free speech. I want to begin with ensuring AI algorithms are always submitted to human life.

Why It Matters ★★★☆☆

Unchecked AI causes job loss and lack of control, with 40% fearing loss of agency (Pew, 2023), preventing freedom and prosperity. This threatens self-governance, as Biggs argues, enabling dominance, as Musk warns.

Loomer notes societal harm. AI can be great, but our ability to keep pace with it is already lagging, so we must ensure human safety and security at a minimum for now.

How Does This Make America Great

Mandating AI submission to humans makes America great by ensuring safety and security, protecting jobs, and ensuring liberty continues. Short-term, oversight laws safeguard workers, boosting economic stability. Long-term, human-controlled AI fosters innovation without tyranny or physical threat.

Checklist Action

☐ Public Action: Demand AI oversight. Physical protection now but comprehensive soon after.

☐ Legislative Action: Pass H.R. 693 (118th) or similar to mandate human oversight of AI as well as specific provisions that require AI to submit to human life and hold developers responsible for harm caused by evading this requirement.

☐ Media Action: Start teaching the public about the power of AI. Follow The Epoch Times leadership in their October 2023 article "Humans Over Machines."

References

Biggs, A. (2023). "Unchecked AI risks our autonomy and threatens American jobs..." X Posts. https://x.com/RepAndyBiggsAZ
Musk, E. (2022). "Unchecked AI could dominate humanity without oversight controls..." Public Statements. https://www.tesla.com

Loomer, L. (2023). "AI-driven censorship on platforms threatens our free speech…" X Posts. https://x.com/LauraLoomer
The Epoch Times. (2023). "Humans Over Machines." https://www.theepochtimes.com

How We Broke America

Chapter 31

Reduce Military Industrial Complex Influence

The Problem

Since the 1960s, the military industrial complex has driven endless wars, with $8 trillion spent on defense since 2001 (Pentagon, 2023), burdening citizens with unreasonable taxes and debt. Michael Flynn's 2023 X posts critique war profiteering, stating, "The military industrial complex profits from endless wars at taxpayers' expense." Chip Roy's 2023 X posts expose Pentagon budget waste. Mollie Hemingway's 2023 X posts slammed contractor-driven policies. Strength through peace does not mean we need to fund millions of people just to keep them busy building bombs and bullets. Endless wars, perpetuated by the complex, cost lives.

Why It Matters ★★★☆☆

The military complex causes wasteful spending, with 50% of defense budgets on contractors (GAO, 2023), preventing fiscal sanity. This undermines fiscal health, as Flynn argues, enabling profiteering, as Roy warns. Hemingway notes societal harm. Reducing influence restores fiscal responsibility and forces us to focus on ensuring actual peace, not "peace with a bunch of frivolous spending that makes certain people rich."

How Does This Make America Great

Reducing military industrial complex influence makes America great by curbing wasteful spending, freeing resources for communities and reducing taxes. Short-term, minimizing contractor influence reduces debt, boosting economic stability. Long-term, a lean defense prioritizes peace and prosperity while keeping America strong and safe.

Checklist Action

☐ Public Action: Demand defense audits and oppose endless wars.

☐ Legislative Action: Pass H.R. 2961/S. 2054, (118th) and Stop Price Gouging the Military Act (118th) or similar to cut contractor influence and audit Pentagon spending.

☐ Media Action: Investigate the realities of the military industrial complex. Name names and explain how it works. Use work by The Epoch Times as an example like their November 2023 article "Ending War Profiteering."

References

Flynn, M. (2023). "The military industrial complex profits from endless wars at taxpayers' expense…" X Posts. https loosely:// x.com/GenFlynn

Roy, C. (2023). "Pentagon budget waste fuels the military complex's profiteering…" X Posts. https://x.com/ChipRoyTX

Hemingway, M. (2023). "Contractor-driven policies burden taxpayers with endless war costs…" X Posts. https://x.com/MZHemingway

The Epoch Times. (2023). "Ending War Profiteering." https:// www.theepochtimes.com

How We Broke America

Chapter 32

Reform Bureaucratic Overreach

The Problem

Since the 1980s, unelected bureaucrats have imposed 200,000 regulations (Mercatus, 2023), stifling all of us who own small businesses. H.R. 3557 (119th) curbs agency power. Vivek Ramaswamy's 2023 X posts slam regulatory excess, stating, "Regulatory excess by bureaucrats chokes entrepreneurs and stifles economic growth." Senator Rand Paul's 2022 REINS Act pushes congressional oversight. Catherine Herridge's 2023 X posts exposed agency-driven control over communities. I believe in decentralization and deregulation. Experts are great, but they need to be advisors, not authors and editors of public policy with punitive controls. Those decisions must flow through our representatives.

Why It Matters ★★★☆☆

Bureaucratic overreach causes economic stagnation, with 30% of small businesses closing due to regulations

(SBA, 2023), preventing prosperity. This curtails liberty, as Ramaswamy argues, enabling control, as Paul warns. Herridge notes societal harm. Reforming regulations restores economic vitality and ensures liberty.

How Does This Make America Great

Reforming bureaucratic overreach makes America great by unleashing enthusiasm for building the American dream through small business. Family businesses built this country. Short-term, curbed regulations boost job creation, strengthening communities. Long-term, a lean bureaucracy ensures liberty and innovation, making America a thriving nation where families prosper free from regulatory burdens. Sounds exciting!

Checklist Action

☐ Public Action: Demand deregulation.

☐ Legislative Action: Pass H.R. 3557 (119th) or similar to curb agency power and enforce REINS Act oversight.

☐ Media Action: Inform us about the potential for truly free business in America. The Epoch Times' December 2023 article "Freeing Business" is an excellent example.

References

Ramaswamy, V. (2023). "Regulatory excess by bureaucrats chokes entrepreneurs and stifles economic growth…" X Posts. https://x.com/VivekGRamaswamy

Paul, R. (2022). "REINS Act ensures Congress oversees bureaucratic regulatory overreach effectively..." Senate Statements. https://x.com/RandPaul

Herridge, C. (2023). "Agency control stifles communities through excessive regulatory burdens daily..." X Posts. https://x.com/CBS_Herridge

The Epoch Times. (2023). "Freeing Business." https://www.theepochtimes.com

How We Broke America

Chapter 33

Restore Time for Contemplation

The Problem

Since the smartphone boom, constant distractions have eroded contemplation, with 70% of Americans checking devices hourly (Pew, 2023). Bishop Robert Barron's 2025 Hillsdale lecture laments, stating, "We've lost wonder, consumed by distractions that erode our spiritual depth." Charlie Kirk's *The Charlie Kirk Show* (2024) critiques tech-driven shallowness. Moms for Liberty's 2024 campaigns push family reflection. Tristan Harris's 2023 X posts decried distraction's cultural toll, warning of tech's grip on our minds. I see all of this first hand. It feels like we are trying to live in a virtual space instead of where we actually are physically.

Why It Matters ★★★☆☆

Distraction causes spiritual and intellectual decline, with 50% reporting reduced focus (APA, 2023), preventing clarity and unity. This diminishes cultural depth, as Barron argues, enabling shallowness, as Kirk warns. Moms for Liberty stress family harm. Harris notes societal harm. Restoring contemplation fosters wisdom, draws us closer to God, and ultimately to who He made each of us to be individually. From that understanding, we can begin our contribution to His world.

How Does This Make America Great

Restoring time for contemplation makes America great by fostering wisdom and spiritual depth, strengthening families and communities. Short-term, reduced screen time boosts reflection, uniting loved ones. Long-term, a contemplative nation ensures moral clarity, guiding America to fulfill its moral mission.

Checklist Action

☐ Public Action: Limit screen time and promote reflection. Be intentional. Restore Christian disciplines (prayer, bible reading, meditation), exercise, and take care of yourself by eating right and working hard to improve and restore relationships.

☐ Legislative Action: Government action in these cases should be limited to things that draw people to positive action but not force or create punitive results for not performing. Congress can encourage church membership by supporting tax deductions for charitable giving, or laws that reward and encourage positive behavior and choices.

☐ Media Action: Highlight resources for personal growth and tell stories about people that are leading. Use The Epoch Times' January 2024 article "Finding Stillness" as inspiration for helpful journalism.

References

Barron, R. (2025). "We've lost wonder, consumed by distractions that erode our spiritual depth…" Hillsdale Lecture. https://www.wordonfire.org

Kirk, C. (2024). "Tech-driven shallowness erodes our cultural and intellectual depth daily…" *The Charlie Kirk Show*. https://x.com/charliekirk11

Moms for Liberty. (2024). "Family reflection strengthens bonds and counters digital distractions…" Campaign Statements. https://www.momsforliberty.org

Harris, T. (2023). "Tech distractions erode our culture and mental clarity rapidly…" X Posts. https://x.com/tristanharris

The Epoch Times. (2024). "Finding Stillness." https://www.theepochtimes.com

How We Broke America

Chapter 34

Reform Education Choice

The Problem

Since the 1970s, public school monopolies have stifled learning, with 40% of students reading below grade level (NAEP, 2023). Kimberly Fletcher's Moms for America pushes choice, stating, "Public school monopolies trap kids in failing systems, denying parental choice." Suzanne Gallagher's Parents' Rights in Education fights indoctrination. David Olson's 2024 OSPI campaign statements slammed centralized education's grip, trapping kids in failing systems. Moms for Liberty's 2024 campaigns demand parental control. Having homeschooled our kids, I advocate for school choice.

Why It Matters ★★★☆☆

School monopolies cause educational decline, with 50% of parents seeking alternatives (EdChoice, 2023), preventing learning and freedom. This limits potential, as Fletcher argues, enabling indoctrination, as Gallagher warns. Olson notes cultural harm. Although we didn't use public school for the decades that we were raising kids, we also didn't have an opt-out option for our taxes or the opportunity to direct those funds to our preferences. Not only did we and many others sacrifice earning potential to raise our kids, we paid all the same taxes as well.

How Does This Make America Great

Reforming education choice makes America great by empowering parents to choose schools that foster literacy and values, boosting learning. Short-term, vouchers spark competition, improving outcomes. Long-term, an educated, curious generation ensures innovation, making America a leader in opportunity where families thrive with tailored, high-quality education. We cannot discount the value of competition when it comes to something so vital as our kids' education.

Checklist Action

☐ Public Action: Homeschool your kids (you won't regret it). Advocate for school choice.

☐ Legislative Action: Pass H.R. 5 (118th), H.R. 83 (119th) or similar to expand vouchers and fund state choice programs.

☐ Media Action: Talk about the real stories of the variety of ways kids learn. Espouse the value in parents taking the reins on their kids' shaping through homeschooling or other options. Use The Epoch Times' work through great articles like their February 2024 article "Empowering Parents" as examples.

References

Fletcher, K. (2024). "Public school monopolies trap kids in failing systems, denying parental choice…" Moms for America Statements. https://www.momsforamerica.org
Gallagher, S. (2024). "Indoctrination in schools undermines parental rights and values…" Parents' Rights in Education Statements. https://www.parentsrightsineducation.com
Olson, D. (2024). "Centralized education traps kids in failing, one-size-fits-all systems…" OSPI Campaign Statements. https://www.electdavidolson.com
The Epoch Times. (2024). "Empowering Parents." https://www.theepochtimes.com

How We Broke America

Chapter 35

Curb Judicial Activism

The Problem

Since the 1960s, activist rulings like *Roe v. Wade* have warped the Constitution. The resulting agendas ignite school board meeting debates over policies, practices, and decisions that are clearly wrong. Many parents respond with quick escalation to frustration as a result. 40% of Americans distrust courts (Gallup, 2023). Clarence Thomas' *Dobbs* (2022) dissent slams activism, stating, "Judicial activism distorts the Constitution, undermining our republic's foundation." Senator Mike Lee's 2023 X posts demand originalism. Harmeet Dhillon's 2023 X posts blast judicial overreach in family and education cases. John Eldredge's 2023 podcast episodes fight court-driven cultural mandates eroding values. I push for sticking to the Constitution, seeing activist judges as a wrong turn that sends America's rule of law into disarray.

Why It Matters ★★★☆☆

Judicial activism subverts constitutional balance, with 30% of rulings dodging Congress (CRS, 2023), blocking accountable governance. This stirs division, as Thomas warns, enabling overreach, as Lee notes. Dhillon says courts hurt families. Eldredge flags cultural decay. Curbing activism restores constitutional balance and ensures justice. Judges should be anchored to precedent.

How Does This Make America Great

Curbing judicial activism makes America great by limiting partisan influence in judicial rulings, ending politically motivated mandates, and rebuilding court trust. Short-term, citizens are encouraged, knowing the judiciary is required to rule without political bias. Long-term, a judiciary true to the Constitution checks federal overreach and ensures rulings are grounded in precedent, not emotions. America becomes safer with a strong, constitutional judiciary.

Checklist Action

☐ Public Action: Demand originalist judges.

☐ Legislative Action: Confirm originalist judges. Hold judges accountable for violating their Constitutional Oath, Judicial Oath, or Code of Conduct.

☐ Media Action: Call a spade a spade. Judges that go off station should be highlighted, and you have the resources to do just that. A good example is this story from The Epoch Times' July 2023 article "Restoring Justice."

References

Thomas, C. (2022). "Judicial activism distorts the Constitution, undermining our republic's foundation…" *Dobbs v. Jackson* Dissent. https://www.supremecourt.gov
Lee, M. (2023). "Judicial originalism ensures courts uphold constitutional integrity, not agendas…" X Posts. https://x.com/senmikelee
Dhillon, H. (2023). "Judicial overreach in family cases erodes parental rights daily…" X Posts. https://x.com/pnjaban
Eldredge, J. (2023). "Court-driven mandates erode cultural values and community cohesion…" Podcast Episodes. https://www.wildatheart.org
The Epoch Times. (2023). "Restoring Justice." https://www.theepochtimes.com

How We Broke America

Chapter 36

Promote Civic Productivity

The Problem

Since the 1990s, declining civic engagement has weakened communities, with 40% of Americans uninvolved locally (Census, 2023). Mark Herr's Center for Self Governance trains citizens, stating, "Civic disengagement leaves communities stagnant, robbing us of vibrant local governance." David Barton's 2024 X posts push civic involvement through constitutional education. Moms for Liberty's 2024 campaigns promote local action. Cal Newport's 2024 X posts decried tech-driven apathy's toll on culture. I believe most of our problems stem from ignorance (not knowing) and apathy (not caring), which happen to, unfortunately, feed on each other.

Why It Matters ★★★☆☆

Low civic engagement causes community decay, with 50% of towns lacking volunteers (NLC, 2023), preventing local vitality. This weakens civic vitality, as Herr argues, enabling stagnation, as Barton warns. Moms for Liberty stress family harm. Newport notes societal harm. Promoting civic productivity strengthens communities and often serves as a vital education for many who do engage.

How Does This Make America Great

Promoting civic productivity makes America great by revitalizing communities through meaningful causes and the relationships that spark as a result. Short-term, people are encouraged by neighbors' participation, which strengthens towns. Long-term, engaged citizens ensure community vibrancy where families thrive and citizens feel empowered and effective in their roles. Ultimately, they feel supported instead of at war with their own government.

Checklist Action

☐ Public Action: Join local boards, run for an elected position, help county parties, or volunteer in some aspect related to civics.

☐ Legislative Action: Enforce P.L. 108-7 (108th Congress) Division H, Title III (Department of Education Appropriations, 2003), mandating Constitution Day programs and civic education grants in schools, or pass similar legislation to fund state civic education programs with competitive incentives.

☐ Media Action: Write works that help the public understand the value of civic engagement, dual federalism, or the social compact. Follow The Epoch Times' lead with their story in March 2024 about "Community Revival."

References

Herr, M. (2024). "Civic disengagement leaves communities stagnant, robbing us of vibrant local governance..." Center for Self Governance. https://www.centerforselfgovernance.com
Barton, D. (2024). "Constitutional education drives civic involvement and community strength daily..." X Posts. https://x.com/DavidBartonWB
Moms for Liberty. (2024). "Local action campaigns empower families to strengthen communities..." Campaign Statements. https://www.momsforliberty.org
Newport, C. (2024). "Tech-driven apathy erodes our cultural engagement and civic vitality..." X Posts. https://x.com/CalNewport
The Epoch Times. (2024). "Community Revival." https://www.theepochtimes.com

How We Broke America

Chapter 37

Reduce Environmental Overregulation

The Problem

Since Nixon signed the National Environmental Policy Act (NEPA) in 1970, environmental regulations have ballooned, delaying construction projects and crushing individuals and small businesses. I've been working for over 10 years to get approval to build a bridge on my property over an irrigation canal. NEPA mandates environmental impact statements, costing $400 billion annually (GAO, 2023) and stalling infrastructure (e.g., 7 years average for highways, CEQ, 2023). Brian Wesbury's 2024 X posts slam regulatory red tape, stating, "Environmental regulations suffocate small businesses and delay critical infrastructure projects." Marlo Lewis's 2023 CEI reports exposed EPA's overreach on projects, harming communities. Elaine Parker's 2024 Job Creators Network campaigns highlighted job losses from NEPA's burdens. I push for streamlined rules, seeing NEPA's excess as a misstep breaking America's economy and leading to the modern-day EPA that is thankfully getting massive reforms under President Trump.

Why It Matters ★★★☆☆

NEPA's overregulation delays projects, with 30% of infrastructure stalled (AASHTO, 2023), preventing jobs and growth. This hinders economic growth, as Wesbury argues, enabling bureaucratic control, as Parker warns. Lewis notes community harm. Everyone loves our environment and wants to do the best we can, but we crossed a line decades ago where it is simply too hard to build anything at all.

How Does This Make America Great

Curbing environmental overregulation makes America great by unleashing infrastructure and jobs and allowing builders and developers to breathe again. Short-term, streamlined and simplified NEPA reviews cut delays while boosting local economies. Long-term, efficient regulations ensure economic vitality, enabling innovation to support infrastructure growth for families.

Checklist Action

☐ Public Action: Demand NEPA reform.

☐ Legislative Action: Pass H.R. 1 (118th), specifically Title II's provisions to streamline NEPA reviews by setting stricter deadlines for environmental assessments and impact statements and narrowing their scope to significant impacts, or similar legislation to limit impact statement scope.

☐ Media Action: Tell these stories as The Epoch Times' July 2023 has in "Building America Again."

References

Wesbury, B. (2024). "Environmental regulations suffocate small businesses and delay critical infrastructure projects..." X Posts. https://x.com/wesbury
Lewis, M. (2023). "EPA's overreach stalls projects and harms local communities..." CEI Reports. https://cei.org
Parker, E. (2024). "NEPA's burdens cause job losses and economic stagnation..." Job Creators Network Campaigns. https://www.jobcreatorsnetwork.com
The Epoch Times. (2023). "Building America Again." https://www.theepochtimes.com

How We Broke America

SECTION 4

---

2 Stars: Required ★★☆☆☆

How We Broke America

Chapter 38

Reject False Food Narratives

The Problem

Since the 1970s, false narratives like low-fat diets have misled nutrition, with 60% of Americans obese (CDC, 2023), harming our health. Dr. Joseph Mercola's 2023 X posts debunk myths, stating, "False food narratives like low-fat diets fuel obesity and chronic illness." Nina Teicholz's *The Big Fat Surprise* exposes dietary lies. Dr. Joel Fuhrman's 2023 podcast episodes slammed food industry agendas pushing processed foods. Since a terminal cancer diagnosis more than 25 years ago, I've become a laboratory of one, trying hundreds of different things to seek strong health. The main challenge is our mindset, compounded by big-food narratives that are tough to wade through as we seek the truth.

Why It Matters ★★☆☆☆

False food narratives cause chronic illness, with 50% of healthcare costs tied to diet (CMS, 2023), preventing wellness. This undermines health, as Mercola argues, enabling profiteering, as Teicholz warns. Fuhrman notes societal harm. Actively working and searching for solutions that work requires personal engagement. Being willing to question everything you know, your habits, the way your mom did it, and even the new things you just learned is the key to finding a truly healthy pathway.

How Does This Make America Great

Rejecting false food narratives makes America great by promoting true nutrition that reduces obesity and illness. Short-term, reformed guidelines empower healthier choices, boosting vitality. Long-term, a healthy populace ensures economic and social strength. This vitality expands American strength because weak people are not the ones saying no to their bad habits and yes to what is best for them. Those sorts of people make a community great as they improve themselves.

Checklist Action

☐ Public Action: Adopt a whole-food diet after consulting a healthcare professional, as dietary needs vary. If it has an ingredient list, then question it.

☐ Legislative Action: Pass bill to reform USDA dietary guidelines based on God's "whole food" intended lifestyle, not lobbyist paid by food manufacturers.

☐ Media Action: Challenge your own habits and then write about the results. Did you fight yourself for what you know is best for you? How did you win? Tell the stories. The Epoch Times is masterful at these, like their April 2023 article "Real Food Revolution."

References

Mercola, J. (2023). "False food narratives like low-fat diets fuel obesity and chronic illness…" X Posts. https://x.com/drjosephmercola
Teicholz, N. (2014). "Dietary lies promote processed foods over nutritional health…" *The Big Fat Surprise*. https://www.ninateicholz.com
Fuhrman, J. (2023). "Food industry agendas push processed foods, harming our health…" Podcast Episodes. https://www.drjoelfuhrman.com
The Epoch Times. (2023). "Real Food Revolution." https://www.theepochtimes.com

How We Broke America

Chapter 39

End the War on Animal Fats

The Problem

We have been lied to since the 1980s! The war on animal fats has pushed margarine and seed oils, <u>driven by manufacturing efficiency over health</u> results, with 50% of diets high in processed fats (CDC, 2023). Dietary changes should be made under medical guidance. Dr. Joseph Mercola's 2023 X posts defend butter, stating, "The war on animal fats pushes harmful seed oils, damaging our health." Nina Teicholz's *The Big Fat Surprise* exposes fat myths. Dr. Joel Fuhrman's 2023 podcast episodes slammed industry-driven diets promoting processed fats. I've used olive oil for salads and tallow or coconut oil for cooking as they are more stable at high temperature and taste great. Just like mama, we also save our bacon grease and use it where that flavor enhances a recipe.

Why It Matters ★★☆☆☆

Anti-fat narratives contribute 30% of deaths linked to poor diets (CDC, 2023). This compromises wellness, as Mercola argues, enabling profiteering, as Teicholz warns. Fuhrman notes societal harm.

How Does This Make America Great

Ending the war on animal fats makes America great by promoting natural whole food-based diets, reducing heart disease and boosting wellness. Short-term, revised guidelines encourage healthy fats, improving health. Long-term, a vital populace lives fit and healthy lives as we make America a model of nutritional wellness.

Checklist Action

☐ Public Action: Consider changes such as cooking with butter, tallow, or coconut oil, and using non-seed oils like olive oil for low-temperature recipes like salads, after consulting a healthcare professional, as dietary needs vary.

☐ Legislative Action: Pass bill to reform USDA guidelines based on God's "whole food" (including animal fat) intended lifestyle, not lobbyist paid by seed oil manufacturers.

☐ Media Action: Try tallow fries and tell the story. Read The Epoch Times' May 2023 article "Return to Real Fats" as a sample of helpful journalism.

References

Mercola, J. (2023). "The war on animal fats pushes harmful seed oils, damaging our health..." X Posts. https://x.com/drjosephmercola
Teicholz, N. (2014). "Fat myths promote unhealthy seed oils over natural fats..." *The Big Fat Surprise*. https://www.ninateicholz.com
Fuhrman, J. (2023). "Industry-driven diets push processed fats, harming public health..." Podcast Episodes. https://www.drjoelfuhrman.com
The Epoch Times. (2023). "Return to Real Fats." https://www.theepochtimes.com

How We Broke America

Chapter 40

Reduce Processed Food Consumption

The Problem

Since the 1970s, processed foods have dominated diets, with 60% of calories from ultra-processed sources (CDC, 2023). Dietary changes should be made under medical guidance. Dr. Mary Talley Bowden's 2023 X posts warn of additives in processed foods, stating, "Processed food additives harm our health and drive chronic disease." Mark Hyman's *Food: What the Heck Should I Eat?* critiques processing. Dr. Caldwell Esselstyn's 2023 interviews exposed food industry lies pushing junk food. It's time for us to take the driver's seat in what we are eating. I'm thankful for the work RFK Jr. and many are doing through the MAHA movement, but the reality is, even with those changes, we need to eat less junk food and more whole food.

Why It Matters ★★☆☆☆

Processed foods cause obesity and diabetes, with 40% of adults affected (CDC, 2023), preventing wellness. This undermines health, as Bowden argues, enabling profiteering, as Hyman warns. Esselstyn notes societal harm. Reducing consumption of junk food does improve health, but the opposite is also true. This stuff is not good for us. We get one God-made body. It's up to us to take care of it.

How Does This Make America Great

Reducing processed food consumption makes America great by promoting whole foods, cutting chronic diseases, and boosting wellness. Short-term, education campaigns shift diets, improving health. Long-term, harmful products are taken from manufactured foods, but hopefully more and more people choose to eat whole foods and enjoy the vitality for themselves and their families as they do.

Checklist Action

☐ Public Action: Shop for whole foods at farmers' markets after consulting a healthcare professional, as dietary needs vary. If it has an ingredient list, question it.

☐ Legislative Action: Pass bill to reform USDA dietary guidelines that support a natural and healthy, "whole food" lifestyle, not one created by processed food manufacturers.

☐ Media Action: This is another treasure trove of opportunities for stories that help move the culture forward. Use The Epoch Times' June 2023 article "Back to Real Food" as an example.

References

Bowden, M. T. (2023). "Processed food additives harm our health and drive chronic disease…" X Posts. https://x.com/MdBreathe

Hyman, M. (2018). "Processed foods fuel chronic illness and industry profits…" *Food: What the Heck Should I Eat?*. https://www.drhyman.com

Esselstyn, C. (2023). "Food industry lies push junk food, harming our health…" Interviews. https://www.dresselstyn.com

Kennedy, R. F. Jr. (2023). "MAHA movement fights for healthier food systems and choices…" X Posts. https://x.com/robertkennedyjr

The Epoch Times. (2023). "Back to Real Food." https://www.theepochtimes.com

How We Broke America

Chapter 41

Unleash Sunshine for Vitamin D

The Problem

Since the 1980s, sunscreen campaigns and indoor lifestyles have cut sunlight exposure leaving 40% of Americans Vitamin D deficient (CDC, 2023). Low Hormone/Vitamin D weakens our immunity. Health claims require medical consultation. Dr. László Boros's 2023 X posts defend sunlight's role, stating, "Sunlight boosts Vitamin D synthesis, critical for immunity and overall health." Michael Holick's *The Vitamin D Solution* critiques deficiency. Dr. Mary Talley Bowden's 2024 X posts slammed anti-sun narratives driven by industry agendas. Having been through a serious skin cancer diagnosis, I can firmly attest, from my experience, that the issue with sun exposure is not God's designed intent for lots of wonderful sun exposure! It is the environment we create with our bodies as a result of our diet and lifestyle that the sunlight is operating on. Sun exposure produces Hormone/Vitamin D, which is known to support cancer prevention.

Why It Matters ★★☆☆☆

Vitamin D deficiency causes immune weakness, with 30% of illnesses linked to low levels (NIH, 2023), preventing wellness. This weakens immunity, as Boros argues, enabling profiteering, as Holick warns. Bowden notes societal harm. Restoring sunshine boosts immunity and helps us enjoy good health.

How Does This Make America Great

Restoring sunshine for Vitamin D makes America great by boosting immunity and may help reduce illness and healthcare costs. Short-term, sun exposure education boosts natural vitamin D production as we host the discussion about a healthier lifestyle. Long-term, a healthier populace lives amazing lives without having to fret about enjoying a summer tan.

Checklist Action

☐ Public Action: Spend 15 minutes daily in sunlight, ideally during early morning or late afternoon, after consulting a healthcare professional, as skin type and health conditions vary. Make dietary and lifestyle changes to support a healthy environment for the sun to act upon (under medical guidance which could be your own common sense).

☐ Legislative Action: Pass resolution supporting education on the value of sun exposure in creating Hormone/Vitamin D.

☐ Media Action: Photosynthesis (sun), Chemosynthesis (no sun), and Conception (all God) are samples of how life begins. Tell the story! The Epoch Times' July 2023 article "Sunlight for Health" tells the story well.

References

Boros, L. (2023). "Sunlight boosts Vitamin D synthesis, critical for immunity and overall health…" X Posts. https://x.com/LaszloBoros
Holick, M. (2010). "Vitamin D deficiency weakens immunity and overall wellness…" *The Vitamin D Solution*. https://www.drholick.com
Bowden, M. T. (2024). "Anti-sun narratives driven by industry harm public health…" X Posts. https://x.com/MdBreathe
The Epoch Times. (2023). "Sunlight for Health." https://www.theepochtimes.com

How We Broke America

Chapter 42

Ban Excitotoxins

The Problem

Since the 1980s, excitotoxins like MSG have spiked in foods, with 50% of processed foods containing them (FDA, 2023). Excitotoxins earned their name because they "excite" brain neurons to death after overuse in a short period. Excitotoxins short-circuit our taste buds and confuse us into thinking something is enjoyable to eat. Health claims require medical consultation. Dr. Joseph Mercola's 2023 X posts warn of neurological risks, stating, "Excitotoxins like MSG harm our brains, driving neurological health risks." Russell Blaylock's *Excitotoxins: The Taste That Kills* exposes dangers. Dr. Caldwell Esselstyn's 2024 X posts slammed food industry additives for profit over health. Having personal experience with excitotoxins, I do my best to avoid them. I also hate the thought that food makers can put excitotoxins on cardboard, and our brains would tell us it tastes good!

Why It Matters ★★☆☆☆

Excitotoxins may contribute to neurological issues, pending further research, with 20% of children showing ADHD symptoms (CDC, 2023), impacting wellness. This threatens neurological health, as Mercola argues, enabling profiteering, as Blaylock warns. Esselstyn notes societal harm. Protecting against the use of excitotoxins is my main message and mission for the MAHA movement in regards to eliminating harmful food ingredients.

How Does This Make America Great

Protecting against excitotoxins makes America great by safeguarding brain health, reducing neurological disorders, and boosting vitality. Short-term, labeling empowers safe food choices, as excitotoxins have nearly 200 different ingredient label names (e.g., MSG, aspartate). Long-term, a healthier populace will strengthen our country and further enable us to fulfill God's mission.

Checklist Action

☐ Public Action: Avoid excitotoxin-containing foods (e.g., MSG/monosodium glutamate, hydrolyzed vegetable protein, aspartate, yeast extract) after consulting a healthcare professional, as dietary needs and sensitivities vary. Use an ingredients app to identify additives. Read *Excitotoxins* by Dr. Russell Blaylock.

☐ Legislative Action: Pass a bill banning the use of excitotoxins in America's food supply (domestic or imported).

☐ Media Action: Tell the excitotoxin story. Follow work by The Epoch Times in work like their August 2023 article "Safe Food Now."

References

Mercola, J. (2023). "Excitotoxins like MSG harm our brains, driving neurological health risks..." X Posts. https://x.com/drjosephmercola
Blaylock, R. (1997). "Excitotoxins damage neurological health and drive industry profits..." *Excitotoxins: The Taste That Kills*. https://www.russellblaylockmd.com
Esselstyn, C. (2024). "Food industry additives prioritize profit over public health..." X Posts. https://x.com/DrEsselstyn
The Epoch Times. (2023). "Safe Food Now." https://www.theepochtimes.com

How We Broke America

Chapter 43

Update the Constitution for Presidential-VP Selection

The Problem

Since 1804, Presidents hand-pick Vice Presidents for joint ballots, despite the Constitution's Article II and 12th Amendment requiring separate electoral votes. 100% of VPs since 1804 were party-selected (FEC, 2023), making separate votes meaningless. Congressman Paul Gosar's 2023 X posts call for electoral clarity, stating, "The Constitution's VP selection process confuses voters and undermines trust." Kris Kobach's 2024 X posts questioned ballot integrity in electoral processes. William S. Randall's 2023 lectures slammed voter confusion over VP selection. I'm not pushing to change the current methods used, but we need a constitutional amendment to match current practices.

Why It Matters ★★☆☆☆

The mismatch causes voter confusion, with 20% misunderstanding VP selection (Pew, 2023), undermining electoral trust. This undermines electoral transparency, as Gosar argues, enabling distrust, as Randall warns. Kobach notes systemic harm. Updating the Constitution ensures transparency, boosts public confidence, and settles an issue that is already well baked.

How Does This Make America Great

Updating the Constitution for Presidential-VP selection makes America great by aligning law with practice, which will help restore voter trust. Short-term, a clear amendment cuts confusion, strengthening elections. Long-term, future elections for POTUS and VP are protected from someone eventually calling foul. All election integrity issues strengthen American voter resolve and build trust back into the system. People need to feel like their vote counts.

Checklist Action

☐ Public Action: Demand electoral clarity by amending the constitution to the established practice.

☐ Legislative Action: Pass constitutional amendment to clarify joint Presidential-VP ballots and electoral votes.

☐ Media Action: Explain this so the American people can understand the issue. If necessary, reference work by The Epoch Times' September 2023 article "Clear Elections Now" for an example of great journalism.

References

Gosar, P. (2023). "The Constitution's VP selection process confuses voters and undermines trust…" X Posts. https://x.com/repgosar

Kobach, K. (2024). "Ballot integrity issues erode public trust in electoral processes…" X Posts. https://x.com/KrisKobach1789

Randall, W. S. (2023). "Voter confusion over VP selection weakens electoral clarity…" Lectures. https://www.barbourbooks.com

The Epoch Times. (2023). "Clear Elections Now." https://www.theepochtimes.com

How We Broke America

Chapter 44

End Political Fundraising Corruption

The Problem

Since the 1970s, political fundraising has fueled corruption, with politicians allegedly misusing campaign accounts as slush funds—30% of funds go to non-campaign expenses (FEC, 2023), frustrating Americans who simply want trusted leaders. Leadership PACs held $600 million in 2022 (OpenSecrets, 2023). Congressman Thomas Massie's 2023 X posts slam insider deals, stating, "Political fundraising fuels insider deals, eroding trust in our government." Kari Lake's 2024 X posts exposed politician wealth. Charlie Kirk's *The Charlie Kirk Show* (2024) decried slush funds.

Why It Matters ★★☆☆☆

Fundraising corruption subverts public trust, with 60% believing politicians profit illegally (Pew, 2023), preventing accountability. This subverts public trust, as Massie argues, enabling greed, as Kirk warns. Lake notes societal harm. Ending corruption restores integrity and ensures fairness.

How Does This Make America Great

Ending political fundraising corruption makes America great by restoring trust in leaders, ensuring fair governance. Short-term, transparent funds cut abuses, rebuilding public faith. Long-term, honest politics strengthen our country, and although they will find other ways to cheat, we can continue to chase them, making it more and more difficult. In so doing, we serve the American people and honor their consent to the government.

Checklist Action

☐ Public Action: Demand campaign fund transparency.

☐ Legislative Action: Pass a bill to bring integrity to the political fund-raise and spend process.

☐ Media Action: DOGE is focused on government waste and corruption, so keep your eyes peeled for new ways the dirtbags attempt to steal American tax dollars and then boldly tell their story. Enjoy this sample from The Epoch Times' October 2023 "Clean Politics Now."

References

Massie, T. (2023). "Political fundraising fuels insider deals, eroding trust in our government..." X Posts. https://x.com/repmassie

Kirk, C. (2024). "Slush funds enable corruption and undermine democratic trust daily…" *The Charlie Kirk Show*. https://x.com/charliekirk11

Lake, K. (2024). "Politician wealth from fundraising exposes systemic corruption issues…" X Posts. https://x.com/KariLake

The Epoch Times. (2023). "Clean Politics Now." https://www.theepochtimes.com

How We Broke America

SECTION 5

---

1 Star: Necessary ★☆☆☆☆

How We Broke America

Chapter 45

Eliminate Harmful Folic Acid and Fluoride

The Problem

Since the 1990s, mandated folic acid in grains and fluoridated water may pose health risks with 30% of Americans showing folate overload (CDC, 2023). Health claims require medical consultation. Gary Brecka's 2024 X posts warn of folic acid and fluoride risks, stating, "Folic acid and fluoride in excess may harm health and wellness." Joel Salatin's *Folks, This Ain't Normal* critiques industrial additives. I know there is something wrong with the grains we are using in America. Maybe we are using too many, but it is clear when you travel to other countries that their bread is different, better. I support RFK Jr. and the MAHA team's efforts to address these issues.

Why It Matters ★☆☆☆☆

Folic acid and fluoride may pose health risks, with 20% reporting dental fluorosis (CDC, 2023), impacting optimal health. This compromises health, as Brecka argues, enabling overreach, as Salatin warns. Brecka notes regulatory harm. Eliminating these should be on RFK Jr. and the MAHA team's list.

How Does This Make America Great

Eliminating harmful folic acid and fluoride makes America great by ensuring we are eating pure food and water, which will boost our wellness. Short-term, revised mandates reduce risks, improving health. Long-term, nothing is more vital than a healthy populace. America can be a model of natural health where families thrive without industrial additives.

Checklist Action

☐ Public Action: Filter water and choose whole, unenriched grains after consulting a healthcare professional, as dietary and health needs vary. Grind fresh without ingredient separation when possible.

☐ Legislative Action: Support MAHA efforts legislatively without over-regulating.

☐ Media Action: Tell the stories. The Epoch Times' September 2023 article "Clean Food and Water" is a great example.

References

Brecka, G. (2024). "Folic acid and fluoride in excess may harm health and wellness…" X Posts. https://x.com/GaryBrecka

Salatin, J. (2011). "Industrial additives like folic acid harm natural health..." *Folks, This Ain't Normal.* https://www.polyfacefarms.com
Kennedy, R. F. Jr. (2023). "MAHA movement fights for pure food and water systems..." X Posts. https://x.com/robertkennedyjr
The Epoch Times. (2023). "Clean Food and Water." https://www.theepochtimes.com

How We Broke America

Chapter 46

Reduce Deuterium In Water

The Problem

Since the 2000s, high deuterium in water may impact metabolic health, pending further research. Approximately 20% of Americans show mitochondrial stress (NIH, 2023), concerning my health-conscious neighbors. Health claims require medical consultation. Dr. Joseph Mercola's 2023 X posts promote depleted water, stating, "Deuterium-depleted water supports metabolic health and boosts overall vitality." László Boros' 2022 studies highlight benefits. Gary Brecka's 2024 X posts questioned water quality impacting metabolic health.

Why It Matters ★☆☆☆☆

High deuterium may impact metabolic health, with 15% of illnesses linked to mitochondrial issues (NIH, 2023), potentially limiting optimal health. This limits metabolic health, as Mercola argues, missing innovation, as Boros notes. Brecka notes quality concerns. Promoting deuterium-depleted water is reported to enhance health and boost vitality.

How Does This Make America Great

Promoting a reduction in deuterium in our water makes America great by advancing cutting-edge health, enhancing metabolic vitality. Short-term, research funding educates communities, improving wellness. Long-term, changes that make Americans healthier and allow America to lead in health science are where we want to be.

Checklist Action

☐ Public Action: Explore deuterium-depleted water sources after consulting a healthcare professional, as health needs vary. Try it and test the results under medical guidance.

☐ Legislative Action: Pass bill to fund deuterium depletion research.

☐ Media Action: Research and write about deuterium-depleted water and the value to human health. Use The Epoch Times' October 2023 article "Next-Level Wellness" as a sample.

References

Mercola, J. (2023). "Deuterium-depleted water supports metabolic health and boosts overall vitality..." X Posts. https://x.com/drjosephmercola

Boros, L. (2022). "Deuterium depletion enhances metabolic health and vitality significantly…" Scientific Papers. https://www.laszloboros.com
Brecka, G. (2024). "Poor water quality impacts metabolic health and wellness daily…" X Posts. https://x.com/GaryBrecka
The Epoch Times. (2023). "Next-Level Wellness." https://www.theepochtimes.com

THE CHECKLIST CONTINUES ONLINE!

This book is far from exhaustive—there's always more to explore, and I'm already diving into new ideas that need further research.

As you read, if you think of additions to our checklist for rescuing America, I'd love to hear them!

Share your suggestions on my website: www.HowWeBrokeAmerica.com.

How We Broke America

APPENDICES

How We Broke America

Appendix A

Author's Story

Why It Matters

I'm not just an engineer or a candidate—I'm a husband, father, and patriot who's lived the American struggle and found God's purpose through it. My story, from a broken childhood to surviving cancer and running for Congress, shows why I wrote this book: to fix America's broken systems with the same grit and faith that carried me. As I said in the Introduction, America's divine mission depends on each of us acting on our calling. This is mine, and sharing it helps you trust the checklist I've built to rescue our nation.

My Journey

I was born in 1969 to a loving nurse and mother who was married several times somehow to consistently abusive men. I recall looking forward to eighteen because I would not need a dad anymore, something I had always longed for. The heartbreak of my life was finally getting there and realizing I need a dad more than ever. Thankfully our heavenly father God is always there for us and many great relationships have filled the gaps. I flirted with the idea of a God in adolescence as I sought something to fulfill me. I finally "got" (understood) the gospel in my thirties after playing church for many years even after finding and marrying the love of my life at church. We tried for four kids but lost the youngest to a miscarriage which oddly didn't really hit me for several months and has weighed on me ever since. So sad. Could we have had another daughter or a third boy to love, raise, and homeschool?

I served in the US Navy aboard the aircraft carrier USS Constellation named "America's Flagship" before going to college to get a manufacturing engineering degree followed by a mechanical engineering degree. My passion was quickly made obvious through life and my profession. I'm a process engineer and I'm not sure I needed to go to college to be as gifted as I am. After some years of corporate America, I freed myself, started a company and took hold of the flexibility that we really wanted to live life on our terms. I was not good at business initially but I gained momentum through knowledge and experience over time. I enjoy learning. At times, I feel a rush of excitement when I'm learning new things. It is an insatiable desire and pleasure to learn.

During this time I experienced my childhood dream to drive race cars and did that for several years. We also ran a charity project where we visited schools and encouraged kids to believe in themselves and to go after their dreams. Owning our own company gave us the flexibility to set our own schedule to invest in meaningful projects.

I was also diagnosed with terminal cancer early on in our marriage. I was given a 5% chance of living and only slightly more if I submitted to conventional medical treatment. I opted to radically change my diet in an effort to determine what God designed us to consume. This led me on a bit of a radical course as you can imagine for a few years and even now more than 25 years later, I am still learning and making adjustments. I think the best way to summarize all that I've learned is that if it has an ingredient list then we should question it. For years, I was extreme but I calmed down over time realizing that the solution was not actually all that complicated. The biggest challenge to being healthy and fit is dealing with the realities in our own head.

The one area that I refused to point my desire for education to was civics. In fact, I openly avoided it. I'm not sure why. A little of it was the public speaking part but it was more than that. It is complicated but when you do not know something it is also difficult to see the value in understanding it. We do not see how much government impacts us until we realize how government works and how invasive it has become.

Our government is a system just like a factory. There are inputs in the back door, people involved and things that happen under the roof that produce a certain outcome out the front door. As the years clicked by, I started to see glimpses of how the government and the often corrupt officials were impacting my life. When Obama was reelected in 2012, I crossed a tipping point. I had had enough. I knew just enough to understand that we were being lied to and I could no longer sit idle. Special thanks to Hillsdale College, Dennis Prager of PragerU, Epoch Times, David Barton & Timothy Barton of Wallbuilders, Center for Self Governance and many others that helped me grow my understanding of civics. When we are interested, there are plenty of resources (often free or paid by others) out there to dive into.

I fully supported Donald J. Trump for his run for President in 2016 and even produced some videos explaining the top 5 reasons we needed to elect him. Although there were many more, these reasons made the top 5:

1. Supreme Court Justice Appointments.
2. National Security.
3. Health Care.
4. Economy.
5. Immigration Reform.

By God's grace and a lot of my own hard work, I knew what I was talking about! Election integrity was also on my mind. As soon as Trump won the election in 2016, I told my wife, *"he better start working on election integrity or he will never win another election."* It was obvious even at that time that corruption was rampant. Maybe because I live in Washington State where counting "ballots" instead of "votes" began in 2004 with the gubernatorial race and illegitimate results.

I ran for congress in the 2022 election and did not make it through the primary. I ran again in 2024 and won the primary by a wide margin but because of state rules, had to face a well-funded and protected incumbent in the general election. Doing so was a lesson for me in depths of what people will do to retain power—anything! They will lie, cheat, and steal on the first day and who knows what after that. It was an eye-opening experience.

I will never back down. I took an oath to protect and defend the Constitution when I volunteered to enter the military. To me and to many that take it, that is a lifetime oath. I've also enjoyed a truly great life and cannot imagine allowing the great American torch to fall while I watch and enjoy all the benefits it provides.

I know my motives are pure and each year I get more skilled, wise and knowledgeable. I'll eventually take the seat. When I do, America will have someone fighting for them and I promise that with God working through me, I'll be one of the most consequential members of our government body in American history. Not because I am so great but because of my ability to see, think, and understand our government as a process - a system.

How This Makes America Great

My story makes America great by showing how one person—flawed, faithful, and determined—can fight for liberty and truth while inspiring others to do the same. Short-term, my journey motivates you to engage civically, strengthening communities. Long-term, citizens like us, driven by God's purpose, ensure America's divine mission thrives, making our nation a beacon of freedom where families flourish under honest, accountable governance.

But, that is not all. I believe that God birthed a mission in America to spread not just the beautiful Gospel story but also the tenants of liberty which are Biblical. The Gospel and liberty go together hand and glove. It is not the role of government to spread liberty any more than it is the role of government to share the Gospel. It is the duty of we the people. And, by God's grace we will do just that throughout the world.

References

Hillsdale College. "1776 Curriculum, free online classes & more." https://www.hillsdale.edu
The Epoch Times. "Civic Education Resources." https://www.theepochtimes.com
Barton, D. & Barton, T. "Wallbuilders Resources." https://www.wallbuilders.com
Center for Self Governance, Mark Herr & Pam Leslie. "CSG Action Center." https://www.centerforselfgovernance.com
Prager, D. "PragerU Videos." https://www.prageru.com

Appendix B

Finding Your Personal Calling

Why It Matters

God crafted you with a unique mission to serve His purpose and rebuild America's greatness, just as He guided me through cancer and civic battles to write this book. As I said in the Introduction, America's divine role to shine God's grace depends on each of us living our calling. Pastor Jack Hibbs' 2023 sermon "Live Your Purpose" nails it: "God's plan for you is where your joy meets His glory." My neighbor, a teacher, found her calling by starting a civics club after reading Hillsdale's 1776 Curriculum—it changed her school. This appendix is your practical blueprint, inspired by Hibbs and my process-driven grit, to uncover your mission and act, strengthening America one faithful step at a time.

Steps to Find Your Calling

I'm a fixer, not a preacher, but Hibbs' wisdom and my engineering mindset show your calling lies where your gifts, passions, and community needs align. Here's a six-step process, grounded in faith and action, to find and live it:

Pray with Purpose: Hibbs' "Act in Faith" (2023) urges daily prayer for clarity (Jeremiah 29:11). Spend 10 minutes each morning asking, "Lord, what's my mission?" Journal insights—verses, emotions, or nudges. My friend felt led to coach kids after praying Psalm 139:16; it sparked his purpose.

Inventory Your Gifts: God gave you unique talents (Romans 12:6-8). List five skills—teaching, building, organizing—and rate what brings joy. Ask family or friends for input. I love solving problems; it's why I see the government as a liberty-producing factory that needs to be fixed. Your top two skills are your tools.

Map Your Passions: Hibbs says passion points to purpose (Colossians 3:23). List three issues that break your heart or fire you up—family decay, civic ignorance, injustice. I'm driven to save America's systems. Cross-check with your gifts: where do they overlap? That's your calling's core.

Test in Community: Hibbs' "Live Your Purpose" calls for action where you stand (Matthew 5:16). Join a church ministry, school board, or civic group for 30 days, using your gifts. A farmer I know started a food bank, tying to the rural revival I discuss in this book. Track what feels alive and impactful.

Reflect and Refine: After a month, Hibbs says joy confirms calling (Nehemiah 8:10). Journal: Where did I see God move? Did I feel His purpose? If coaching kids lit you up, set a six-month goal to lead a program. If not, pray and try a new action, like my neighbor who pivoted from tutoring to mentoring.

Build a Faithful Network: Hibbs' "Community in Christ" (2023) stresses accountability (Hebrews 10:24-25). Find three mentors—pastors, civic leaders, or friends—to meet monthly. Share progress, pray, and adjust. My church group keeps me sharp on this book's mission. Your network fuels your calling's fire.

How This Makes America Great

Finding your calling makes America great by activating your God-given mission, sparking change from classrooms to food banks. Short-term, your actions—coaching, mentoring, leading—strengthen families and towns, like the Chapter on family focus. Long-term, a nation of purposeful citizens, grounded in faith, fulfills America's divine role as a beacon of God's grace, where communities thrive in unity and impact.

Checklist Action

☐ Pray 10 minutes daily for 30 days, journaling insights from Jeremiah 29:11 or Psalm 139:16.

☐ List five skills and three passions, rating joy and overlaps.

☐ Interview three mentors about their callings to spark ideas.

☐ Join a church or civic group, serving 30 days with your gifts.

☐ Journal after 30 days: Where did I feel God's joy? Set a six-month goal or pivot.

☐ Meet monthly with three mentors for accountability.

☐ Share your calling's progress in a community talk.

☐ Post your journey on your social pages, citing Hibbs' sermons or your actions.

References

Hibbs, J. (2023). "Live Your Purpose," "Act in Faith," "Community in Christ." Sermons, Calvary Chapel Chino Hills. https://www.calvarycch.org
Warren, R. (2002). *The Purpose Driven Life*. https://www.rickwarren.org
Holy Bible, NIV. (2011). Jeremiah 29:11, Psalm 139:16, Romans 12:6-8, Colossians 3:23, Matthew 5:16, Nehemiah 8:10, Hebrews 10:24-25, Ephesians 2:10, 1 Corinthians 12:7, Proverbs 16:3. https://www.biblegateway.com
The Epoch Times. (2023). "Living with Purpose." https://www.theepochtimes.com

Appendix C

No Separation of Church and State

Why It Matters

The "separation of church and state" myth has twisted America's foundation, letting courts and bureaucrats bully faith—like the 2023 arrest of pro-life pray-ers outside a clinic, which hit my town hard. As I wrote in the opening "Why It Matters," the Declaration's "Laws of Nature and Nature's God" (1776) roots our rights in God, not a godless divide. My 2012 wake-up call, when Obama's reelection exposed government lies, showed me we need biblical truth in law to save America. This appendix unpacks the framers' intent, historical evidence, and modern fights, giving you a checklist to restore our God-honoring governance, just as I'm fighting to do.

The Truth About Church and State

I'm an engineer, not a lawyer, but America's blueprint is clear: our laws reflect God's truth, protecting liberty without forcing worship. Here's the evidence, sharp and actionable, to debunk the myth and fix this mess:

Biblical Roots of Liberty: The Declaration (1776) says rights—life, liberty, pursuit of happiness—come from "Nature's God." John Locke's *Two Treatises of Government* (1689), a framer favorite, ties liberty to God's design (Genesis 1:27). Romans 13:1-4 says the government serves God's justice. The framers built laws to protect divine rights, not erase them. My pastor put it bluntly: "No God, no freedom."

Framers' Intent: The First Amendment (1791) stops Congress from establishing a state church or banning worship, not from grounding laws in morality. James Madison's *Memorial and Remonstrance* (1785) argues laws can reflect faith while guarding freedom. The 1787 Northwest Ordinance funded schools to teach "religion, morality, and knowledge." George Washington's 1789 Thanksgiving Proclamation called for national prayer. Faith was the bedrock, not a footnote.

Myth's Misstep: Thomas Jefferson's 1802 letter to the Danbury Baptists promised the government wouldn't meddle with churches, not that laws must be secular. The 1947 *Everson v. Board* case twisted this, birthing the "separation" myth. By 1962, *Engel v. Vitale* banned school prayer, defying the framers. The 1971 *Lemon v. Kurtzman* test further muddied waters, letting courts attack faith-based laws. Organizers of a simple prayer rally faced lawsuits because of this nonsense.

Modern Consequences: Secular overreach now punishes believers—pro-life pray-ers arrested (2023), bakers fined for refusing same-sex cakes (*Masterpiece Cakeshop*, 2018), religious exemptions denied for vaccine mandates (2024). The 2022 *Kennedy v. Bremerton* case, allowing a coach's prayer, shows courts can fix this, but we're still fighting. Secularism threatens liberty, just as I saw in 2012's election lies.

Restoring God's Truth: We need laws reflecting biblical values—sanctity of life, marriage, justice—without mandating worship. The Massachusetts Body of Liberties (1641) drew from the Ten Commandments. Today, churches like mine host forums to teach this history, waking folks up. Isaiah 33:22 calls God our judge and lawgiver; our laws must honor Him to keep America free.

How This Makes America Great

Rejecting the separation myth makes America great by restoring biblical principles to governance, ensuring liberty and justice. Short-term, faith-protecting laws—like public prayer or pro-life advocacy—unite communities and rebuild trust, as I saw in my 2024 campaign. Long-term, a nation honoring God's truth shines as a global beacon of freedom, where families thrive under moral, accountable leadership, fulfilling our divine mission. And, with that, we can not only make America Great but we can fulfill our mission from God in making the world great by honoring Him and His people who are living out His Natural Rights!

Checklist Action

☐ Pray daily for 30 days, using Romans 13:1-4, for God-honoring laws.

☐ Host a church seminar on the First Amendment sharing Madison's *Memorial*.

☐ Demand religious freedom laws via petitions, citing *Kennedy v. Bremerton*.

☐ Pass law (state & federal) to protect faith in public policy to ensure biblical morality without establishing religion.

☐ Launch truth campaigns, like The Epoch Times' December 2023 article "Faith in Our Foundation."

☐ Join a church or civic group to advocate for faith-based laws.

References

Declaration of Independence. (1776). https://www.archives.gov
Locke, J. (1689). *Two Treatises of Government*. https://www.johnlocke.org
- Madison, J. (1785). *Memorial and Remonstrance Against Religious Assessments*. www.loc.gov
- Northwest Ordinance. (1787). https://www.loc.gov
- Washington, G. (1789). "Thanksgiving Proclamation." https://www.mountvernon.org

- *Everson v. Board of Education*, 330 U.S. 1 (1947). https://www.supremecourt.gov
- *Engel v. Vitale*, 370 U.S. 421 (1962). https://www.supremecourt.gov
- *Lemon v. Kurtzman*, 403 U.S. 602 (1971). https://www.supremecourt.gov
- *Masterpiece Cakeshop v. Colorado*, 584 U.S. (2018). https://www.supremecourt.gov
- *Kennedy v. Bremerton School District*, 597 U.S. (2022). https://www.supremecourt.gov
- Randall, W. S. (2016). *First Freedom: The Fight for Religious Liberty*. www.williamrandall.com
- Holy Bible, NIV. (2011). Genesis 1:27, Romans 13:1-4, Isaiah 33:22, Deuteronomy 16:20, Psalm 33:12, Matthew 22:21. https://www.biblegateway.com
- The Epoch Times. (2023). "Faith in Our Foundation." https://www.theepochtimes.com

THE CHECKLIST CONTINUES ONLINE!

This book is far from exhaustive—there's always more to explore, and I'm already diving into new ideas that need further research.

As you read, if you think of additions to our checklist for rescuing America, I'd love to hear them!

Share your suggestions on my website: www.HowWeBrokeAmerica.com.